Sales and Marketing Careers in the Tech Sector

David K. Wolpert

Swordfish Communications
Austin, Texas

Published by Swordfish Communications, LLC
www.SwordfishCommunications.com

ISBN-13: 978-097419553-7

Library of Congress Control Number: 2007908232

First edition, January 2008

Contents

Preface

I like to write books that I wish I could have read earlier in my life. The genesis for this book dates back to September 1997, when I attended a career fair two weeks after starting the MBA program at the University of Texas. All I knew was that I needed to secure a summer internship. I didn't particularly care which industry I worked in or precisely what I did. At that point, I had three years of experience in information technology and consulting under my belt, and jobs with technology companies were all the rage.

As I wandered around the job fair, I saw a table for Compaq Computer (now Hewlett-Packard). I approached the recruiter and asked her if Compaq was looking to hire summer interns. "Of course," she said. "What area are you interested in?"

I must have looked like a deer in headlights. I really hadn't given it any thought. I didn't even know what my options were. And so I asked a question recruiters really hate to hear.

"Well, what positions do you have?"

I could tell the recruiter wasn't pleased. "Sir, we have over 3,500 open positions. What department are you most interested in?"

"Um…marketing?" In hindsight, I don't know where I pulled that answer out of. As an undergraduate, I had taken one marketing course, and I had always been interested in the marketing side of business. But I really didn't know what "marketing" was all about. I couldn't even define it well. But by process of elimination, marketing sounded better to me than, say, accounting or finance.

The recruiter was clearly annoyed. With a firmer tone, she explained, "We have a few hundred marketing positions available. What, specifically, do you want to do?"

Having by now clearly blown my chances of securing a job with Compaq, I felt I had nothing to lose by continuing this naïve line of questioning.

"Well...what kinds of marketing positions are available?"

The patient recruiter began to rattle off job categories – product marketing, brand management, channel management, partner relations, corporate communications, PR, and others – and I had absolutely no idea what she was talking about. I left the job fair defeated. I clearly had a lot to learn.

Ten years later, I finally *do* know what she was talking about. And as I moved from tech company to tech company during the boom, then bust, then recovery, I've had the benefit of holding several job titles and working with people in all the other business fields found in the tech sector.

Over those ten years, I've come to meet a lot of people who remind me of myself at that job fair: undergraduates seeking internships, recent college graduates looking for a first job, experienced professionals considering a career change into the tech sector, people already working for a technology company but interested in learning more about other career options, and even people who are just curious what all these tech people do for a living. If you fall into these categories, this book is for you.

Note that there are quite a few books and websites that will help you in actually landing these jobs. For that, there are dozens of books, articles and great websites about how to write a resume, interviewing techniques, professional networking, and many more related topics.

Finally, I must thank several individuals who provided invaluable assistance on this book: Thomas Aitchison, Jake Angerman, Chris Boyd, Alison Cowden, Ann Dahlquist, Gaea Connary, Amanda Finch, Julie Humble, Cheryl Klinginsmith, and Cindy Lo.

I sincerely hope that this book helps you find the job that's right for you.

– David Wolpert

Sales and Marketing Careers in the Tech Sector

CHAPTER ONE

So, You Want to be in Tech?

For those who have never worked in it, the "tech sector" can be a strange and wondrous place. It's a world full of interesting companies, fascinating people, amazing products, and great career opportunities. Sometimes.

Defining "Tech"

What makes a company a tech company? This is a tricky question, because there is no precise definition of what kinds of companies the "tech sector" includes. The term "tech" *usually* applies to companies in the computer software and hardware market, though this distinction is increasingly blurry. For instance, Apple used to make only computer hardware and some software – thus making it unquestionably a "tech" company by a computer-centric definition – but today the company also makes consumer electronics such as the iPod and iPhone and recently removed the word "Computer" from its company name.

Historically, in many cases the term "tech company" also implied that the company offered a tangible product, which could be computer equipment, a software program, or even a website. Today, many tech companies derive a substantial portion (in some cases a majority) of their revenue from services, not products. IBM may derive more revenue from sales of computer hardware and software than from services, but its service offerings probably employ more people, are more profitable, and grow revenue faster than its product groups.

Would Apple and IBM still be considered tech companies? For the purposes of this book, yes – because these companies tend to organize their staff and define job functions similarly. In fact, regardless of the specific product and service offered, the majority of companies that are substantially involved in computer hardware, software of any kind, or Internet-related software and services tend to have more similarities than differences when it comes to staffing.

What about other kinds of technology-driven companies? The short answer is, it depends. Consider an upstart company that's pioneering a new way to make solar panels. The product is clearly "high tech." The question, though, is to what extent such a company would be organized similar to, say, a software company. In general, the earlier stage such a company is, the less it would resemble a tech company as defined in this book. Why? Because an early stage, "super high tech" company will primarily employ scientists and engineers and not yet have a salable product. If the product isn't quite ready to be sold, there's no need for sales or marketing staff.

What's Hot, What's Not in Tech

Like every industry, working in the tech sector has pros and cons. It's definitely not for everyone. Some of the positives include:

Job growth remains strong. According to a study released by AeA[1], a technology industry trade association, in 2006 tech companies added nearly 150,000 jobs in the United States. That's nearly double the number of jobs added in 2005. Today, approximately 5.8 million people in the United States work in tech – the highest number since 2002, when most of the "dot-com boom" was still booming.

However, some industries within the tech sector are growing faster than others, while some are shrinking. Again, according AeA, in 2006, software companies added the most jobs (about 88,500) while semiconductor manufacturers added 10,900 positions. But computer and peripheral equipment makers cut 6,200 jobs. Of course, these figures represent total employment – not just in Sales or Marketing. Even when an industry is shrinking overall, there may still be lucrative employment opportunities, especially at smaller companies.

Permanence. The tech sector isn't going anywhere. Computers have become such an ingrained part of our world that it's hard to imagine the tech sector ever disappearing. Moreover, while specific jobs may come and go based on shifts in technology, there will always be a need for sales and marketing professionals.

Salaries at every level tend to be higher than similar jobs in other industries. According to the AeA, in 2005 wages at tech companies

---

[1] *Cyberstates 2007: A Complete State-by-State Overview of the High-Technology Industry*. See www.aeanet.org.

nationwide averaged $75,500. That's 86 percent more than the average private-sector wage of $40,500.

Culturally, tech companies tend to be very laid back. Dress code norms range from completely casual to business casual but, except for some customer-facing positions, rarely require dressing up. People are generally friendly and supportive of one another. Most tech companies provide their employees with free food and other perks.

Flexible working arrangements. There's an attitude at most tech companies that it doesn't matter when or where you work as long as the work gets done. Armed with nothing more than a high-speed Internet connection, a laptop and a cell phone, most Sales and Marketing professionals can perform most of their work anywhere, anytime. As such, tech employers are more lenient than those in most other industries when it comes to employees' desires about living in a particular city, working certain hours, and telecommuting from home.

American tech companies are clustered in some very nice places to live. Bigger, move livable cities like San Francisco, Boston, Seattle, and a lot of college towns like Austin.

What's *not* to like about working in tech? Well…

Chaotic work. Technologies change quickly and often, and tech companies may need to radically alter their courses to respond to the introduction of new technologies or new competitors. You can get caught in the crossfire. You may have been working on a project for months, and then one day come in to the office to find that the project was just cancelled because a competitor you've never heard of launched a threatening new product overnight.

Companies come and go. Just as products come and go, so do tech companies. The industry is constantly in flux, with mergers, acquisitions, and dissolutions all over the place. Job security in tech is tenuous, especially at smaller companies.

The work is tough. This is certainly not true at all tech companies, but at many companies, people work extremely long hours and may be required to travel extensively. Younger folks just starting out in their careers may not mind this, but it can be tough on families.

There's also a phenomenon I would describe as being overly connected. Since most people in tech are armed with a laptop, high-speed Internet connection and cell phone, it's very easy for other people to reach you – and they inevitably will, even during evenings and weekends or while you're away on vacation. Likewise, I know few people in tech who can resist the temptation to at least occasionally check their work email or voice mail at odd hours of the night and on weekends. It can be hard – sometimes by choice, sometimes by necessity – to separate work from the rest of your life.

Is Tech Still Sexy?

In the late 1990s, tech companies understandably had an aura of sexiness. In those days, venture capital firms were pouring tens of billions of dollars into start-ups founded by twenty-somethings who generally had little more than an interesting business idea. Arrogance and delusion were rampant. And spend those billions they did. Many of these upstarts hired far more people than they needed, often at truly ridiculous salaries, and showered employees with stock options, cool offices, and perks like the latest cell phone, over-the-top weekly beer bashes, and company parties in Hawaii. No one could argue that those weren't fun days and, yes, working in tech was sexy.

My, how quickly industry changes. Today, shadows of the go-go days of tech are still with us, but for the most part the entire sector has come back down to earth. Venture capital firms now prefer to invest in later-stage companies that have proven they can build and sell products. Wall Street expects companies seeking to go public to be profitable (or demonstrably on their way there) and have seasoned management teams. And all tech companies have restrained their extravagant spending on gadgets, parties and whole-company trips.

Deciding Whom to Work For

As you consider joining a tech company, there are a few things you should consider.

Hardware vs. Software

What a company primarily makes (hardware, software, or services) impacts the company's culture and one's career opportunities.

Compared to most software vendors, companies that manufacture products tend to be slower-moving, more bureaucratic organizations. Manufacturing requires longer product development lead times than software, because creating software does not involve the complexities of production, certification, distribution and other steps necessary to bring a physical product to the market. (Selling "shrink-wrapped" software through a retail chain requires some of the same basic steps, but each step is generally simpler than that for producing, say, a computer monitor.) Since most technology product manufacturing is now performed at least in part overseas, hardware companies are usually international from their start. Hardware companies tend to have a pervasive, relentless goal to drive down manufacturing costs by whatever means possible.

Software companies tend to be "lighter on their feet" than hardware companies, for a few reasons. First, they generally do not have a "supply chain" (manufacturing, warehousing, distribution, etc.). As such, software companies tend to be smaller than hardware companies, with fewer departments and overall staffing levels. Second, software products are easier to copy and bring to market than physical goods, so software companies are under continuous pressure to develop new or improved products, and to respond quickly in turbulent competitive environments.

What does this mean from a sales and marketing career standpoint? Well, the larger size and scope of hardware companies typically means more career options and mobility, with more facilities throughout the world, and more jobs to fill. The majority of U.S.-based software companies are too small to have offices throughout the world and, when they do, they tend to be small "satellite" offices staffed only with a handful of sales, sales engineering, and regional marketing personnel. You could start a career in marketing with a hardware manufacturer based in California, temporarily be assigned to work in its manufacturing operations in Singapore, and then later move to a regional sales office in London.

Location
When thinking about beginning a new career, a big part of the decision is where you wish to reside. Most tech companies have distributed Sales teams (spread across the country), so regardless of where the company is based you may be able to join a Sales team anywhere in the country. Even so, you would probably need to visit the headquarters office several times per year for training. For Marketing positions, you will almost certainly need to be based at the company's headquarters, at least until you have proven yourself at the company and have amassed the skills and reputation to be able to work remotely.

Some industries are clustered in certain areas. Dallas, for example, has a high concentration of companies in the telecom hardware, software and services sector. The Washington, D.C. area has a large number of software companies focused on developing software for U.S. Government agencies. San Francisco is more software- and Internet-focused, with few hardware companies. Cities like Austin, Texas and San Jose, California have a more balanced mix of software, hardware and other tech industries. With the exception of the more balanced regions, choosing an area to live in and choosing what side of the tech industry you will work for are integral decisions.

It's also worth considering that the tech sectors in some regions are growing faster than others. According to the AeA, in 2005, in order, the fastest growing states by tech employment were California, Texas, New York, Florida and Virginia.

Finally, different regions have different cultures, and the culture of the tech firms within them is not immune from this.

Size of the Company

There are pros and cons to joining a smaller versus a larger company in a sales or marketing capacity, and these aren't necessarily unique to tech.

Marketers in small companies are almost always generalists. They will have the opportunity to do a bit of everything. If you're the type of person who learns best by being thrown into a fire and asked to figure it out, this can be a great way to learn about all aspects of marketing. And, in my experience, marketers who are well-versed in all aspects of marketing tend to get promoted faster than those who specialize. On the other hand, by working in a smaller company you will gain breadth but not depth. Many companies, especially mid-sized ones, look for people with some modicum of "deep experience" in one area.

In Sales, the toss-up is that at a small company any one salesperson can shine, whereas at a larger company that has more salespeople, it's harder to stand out. The key is the average deal size. A lower-performing salesperson at a giant tech company may earn more than the star performer at a smaller one, simply because the larger company sells much more expensive products.

B-to-B vs. B-to-C

These acronyms refer to businesses that sell their products to other businesses (B) versus to consumers (C). Some companies, like Dell, do both; they sell computers to corporations as well as to the general public. Companies that only sell to one of the two have subtle but important distinguishing aspects.

To be good at sales or marketing in a B-to-B company, you need to be able to "get into the heads" of your target industry customers. You'll need to learn the unique jargon of their business, articulate product features and benefits in their terms, and focus more on the business case and financial reasons why they should buy your products. Selling or marketing to consumers is a little different. Suppose your company makes an anti-virus software tool. Persuading the general public to buy it for their home computer is a different game than convincing information technology directors at Fortune 500 companies to buy it. The product is the same, but the marketing strategies and tactics and the entire sales approach is quite different. In fact, an increasing number of products sold to consumers aren't sold by salespeople at all; the products may be sold through the company's website, or through retail channels, for instance.

Companies that sell "commodity products" – well-established products that customers have already embraced and tend to choose based on price or brand alone – generally resemble B-to-B companies, even if consumers are a significant target market. The personal computer falls into this category. Computers are so commonplace today that no one needs to be educated on what a computer is or why it's useful. And the computer industry is well-established, so few new companies are getting into this market. As a result, selling and marketing computers has become largely a game of reinforcing one vendor's brand image or promoting the specific mix of features or low price of one model over another.

Market-Driven vs. Sales-Driven Organizations

Technology companies tend to follow one of two cultural philosophies. One is that the products and services they develop should be based on input from "the market" – what current or prospective customers and industry experts of various kinds believe is needed. Market-driven companies invest in market research and base product decisions on data and other forms of information. In market-driven companies, Marketing departments have enormous value because they "front-end" the product definition process. One downside to market-driven companies is that they make decisions more slowly, which in a fast-moving industry may prove fatal.

In contrast, a sales-driven organization makes decisions based on a simple question: Can we sell that? In such a company, product development decisions are often driven by the Sales organization, or by a visionary executive (often the CEO or Founder) who relies on intuition, not market feedback, to guide what gets built, how it's priced, and how it's sold.

It's impossible to say which philosophy is superior. From a job seeker's standpoint, I'd suggest that if you're more analytical by nature, you might be happier with the approach taken by market-driven companies. If you place a higher value on expediency, a sales-driven culture might be more to your liking. More generally, marketers will be able to add more value in a market-driven company, and salespeople will add more value in a sales-driven company.

The Jobs Covered in This Book

The remainder of this book contains detailed profiles of the most common Marketing and Sales positions in tech companies. Of course, there are a lot of variations out there. Even so, while it's impossible to be accurate on this point, I estimate that 90% of tech companies in the United States would match with at least 80% of what's in these descriptions. Put differently, run these descriptions by anyone who has been in a Sales or Marketing role with a tech company for a few years, and they'll probably tell you that the descriptions are "mostly right."

The inventory of job profiles in this book is by no means exhaustive. Tech companies are notorious for creating odd-sounding job titles in an effort to differentiate themselves from other tech companies. These oddball titles can also serve to attract strong candidates to positions in which the work is fairly dull. Read job descriptions carefully and with a discriminating eye, and try to match descriptions you see with the profiles in this book. What one company calls "Market Development" may just be "Inside Sales" to 90% of other companies out there.

Matching Jobs to Your Background

If you...	Consider...
Have a technical background	Product Marketing or Product Management, Sales Engineering
Are a strong writer	Product Marketing, MarCom, CorpComm, PR
Have strong quantitative skills	Product Marketing or Product Management, Marketing Programs, Sales Operations
Have strong interpersonal skills	Inside or Outside Sales, Sales Engineering, Market Development
Recently graduated from college	Inside Sales, Events

CHAPTER TWO

The Marketing Organization

Defining Marketing

If you ask one hundred marketers to define marketing, you will get *at least* one hundred answers. Marketing is hard to define because the range of activities in which a typical Marketing department is involved is so broad.

Most definitions tend to fall into one of two camps. Either they're a bit on the "fluffy" side, like, "marketers are the protectors of a company's image and reputation." Or, you find definitions that, frankly, make marketing sound really boring to most people, if not a little hard to readily grasp. The American Marketing Association defines marketing as,

> "The process of planning and executing the conception, pricing, promotion and distribution of ideas, goods and services to create exchange and satisfy individual and organizational objectives."

Hmm. I prefer a definition quoted in the book, *High-Tech Careers for Low-Tech People*:

> "Marketing is doing everything you have to do to sell the product except actually getting out there and selling it."

You could phrase it differently to say that Marketing *enables* the Sales team. Everything Marketing does, directly or indirectly, helps drive sales.

I also like the way Peter Bowerman, an author of a book about how to self-publish a book (I know, that has nothing to do with the tech sector), contrasts sales and marketing. Sales, he says, involves direct contact with a customer, usually in person or by phone. Marketing, he contrasts, is primarily about generating awareness of the company and its products, and doing so in less personal ways, such as by direct mail or advertising. Successful marketing, he writes, "involves letting your various audiences....know you're out there— on a consistent basis, in a variety of ways, and with a message they can hear that cuts through the clutter."

Of course, not everything marketers do is about *sending* messages to the market. The flip side of Marketing is *receiving* messages – learning about what current and prospective customers want, studying what competitors are doing, and collecting information from a variety of sources to predict future trends and market needs. This concept of sending versus receiving is called *outbound* compared to *inbound* marketing, respectively, or "being the voice of the company" compared to "being the voice of the customer."

As you read through the chapters on what marketers do, you'll notice overlap across these lines, in some roles more than others. Product Marketers, for example, typically balance their time between inbound marketing activities (for example, meeting with prospective customers to learn about their future product needs) and outbound activities (such as creating marketing materials). A Public Relations Manager, in contrast, spends almost all of his or her time on outbound activities like writing press releases.

Job Titles in Tech Marketing

In the tech sector, job titles are everything. Marketing titles are more standardized than in Sales, but there are plenty of exceptions. This section outlines the most common titles.

One general way roles are segmented is with the term "individual contributor" (IC). Simply put, ICs perform more tactical work and are less involved (if at all) in more strategic activities such as long-range planning or budgeting.

Intern. Interns are usually undergraduate students who work either part-time during their school year (usually Junior or Senior year) or full-time over the summer between their Junior and Senior years in college.

Interns are not employees. They are usually paid at an hourly rate and receive no benefits (health care coverage, etc.). The hourly rates can be low and are not usually negotiable; typical Intern rates for Marketing positions range from $8 to $12 per hour, but again there are exceptions. Still, Interns at tech companies *usually* earn more than working in retail sales or other jobs commonly held by undergraduates.

Marketing Interns are usually paired up with professionals on the MarCom side of the Marketing house, particularly in the PR, Marketing Programs Management, and Events functions. For Interns, this makes sense, because these areas are more tactically, output driven functions to which someone with minimal training or experience can make a significant and welcome contribution. Interns do things such as checking venue availability for company events, purchasing and mailing gifts to key customers, and coordinating the logistics for media interviews. It may not sound particularly exciting, but the contributions Interns make is very much welcome by the rest of the Marketing staff.

Coordinator or **Associate**. A Marketing Coordinator or Associate is one step up from an Intern and *is* an employee. These individuals typically have completed a Bachelor's degree and have at most two or three years of related work experience. Individuals hired into a tech company from another industry might start with this title even if they have many more years of total work experience.

Coordinators and Associates are traditional entry-level positions. Individuals in these roles may do any type of work, but generally work closely under a more experienced Manager or Director. Undergraduate students who performed well at the company as an Intern are often offered a job as a Coordinator or Associate upon graduation.

Specialist and **Manager**. The title of Manager highlights an interesting quirk in tech sector titles. In most industries, the term "Manager" implies that an individual has direct reports – people reporting to you, meaning you direct what they work on and also conduct their performance evaluations. But in tech, most Managers in Marketing positions do not have anyone directly reporting to them. In tech marketing, the term "Manager" refers to managing products, processes, campaigns, territories, budgets and the like, but not people.

Even so, it is not uncommon for a more senior Marketing Manager to have one or two people reporting to him or her in an informal capacity. This might be done to "groom" the Manager for a Director-level position in which he or she will manage people, or simply to divide up the work of managing a large Marketing team's activities. Managers who informally manage others may also be given a title such as "Team Lead."

Some tech companies draw a distinction between Manager and Specialist to reflect whether the individual has direct reports. In these companies, Managers and Specialists do basically the same work, but Managers have direct reports and Specialists do not.

Another variant title is Senior Manager. This signifies that an individual has more experience than a typical Manager, even though the work Senior Managers do generally isn't different from what Managers do. The title of Senior Manager is often given to an individual as a "promotion" from Manager. On a resume, this suggests career progression; in reality, it mainly indicates tenure.

Regardless of the exact title, most individuals at the Marketing Manager level have four to eight years of related work experience, or have an advanced degree such as an MBA.

Director. In tech company Marketing organizations, the title of Director almost universally signifies that the individual has direct reports, or will in the foreseeable future. Compared to a Manager, Directors typically perform more strategically-oriented work; Directors and higher-level positions are not considered individual contributors. Because they have direct reports, Directors need to allocate time to develop the careers of their team members.

One common exception to this is that in early-stage start-up companies where there is no Marketing staff, the first Marketer hired is frequently hired in as a Director. This individual is then either promoted to VP when the company gains traction in the market, or left in that position to build a Marketing team while a search for a VP is conducted.

Vice President and **Chief Marketing Officer**. In small- to mid-sized tech companies, Vice President (VP) is the highest title one can usually attain in Marketing. Smaller tech companies typically have one VP who oversees the entire Marketing function, with all Directors and occasionally the more senior Managers reporting to him or her. Larger companies may have "parallel" VPs who oversee groups of Marketing functions, such as a VP of Product Marketing and a VP of Marketing Communications. In this case, all the Marketing VPs may report to a Chief Marketing Officer (CMO) who has responsibility for the entire Marketing function.

Some tech companies have a CMO to signify that the Marketing function is recognized as being equally important as other functions that usually have a C-level officer, such as the CEO (Chief Executive Officer), CFO (Financial), and CTO (Technology).

Most VPs or CMOs have 10 to 20 years of experience, or fewer years of experience but have proven their value by making significant contributions to the Marketing functions at other companies. Many also have MBAs.

The Two Sides of Tech Marketing

Marketing roles in tech companies can be roughly divided into two groups: the product side and the marketing communications ("MarCom") side.

The "product" (sometimes called "solutions") side of the house includes product marketing, product management (if part of Marketing), field marketing, market development, segment marketing, partner marketing, and competitive analysis. Individuals in these roles tend to be more technical and interact with customers (in Marketing jargon, they are said to be "customer-facing").

The MarCom side of the house consists of people in online marketing, events management, marketing programs management, corporate communications, and any number of writers, editors and graphic designers. Individuals in these roles tend to have strong communications skills and are *not* usually customer-facing.

Of course, not all tech companies have individuals in all these roles. Generally, the smaller the company, the more likely the Marketing staff are generalists whose work touches on all these areas. In a very small company, the entire Marketing staff may just be one person. But as the company grows, there will typically be some specialization along the two sides outlined above. The earliest hires may all report to one Director or VP of Marketing, but as the team grows, most companies will hire or promote, for example, a Director of MarCom and a Director of Product or Solutions Marketing. Later, those two teams may be further segmented or spun-off. For instance, Corporate Communications may become its own group either within Marketing or in a new, completely separate department. Or, when a company's product portfolio becomes broad, Product Marketing may become its own group, led by a dedicated Director of Product Marketing.

Jobs Not Covered in this Book

There are a few marketing roles that are not covered in this book, either because they are fairly rare or because they are similar to or subsets of other fields. These include:

- **MarCom** (Marketing Communications) is a catch-all term for marketing roles that don't fall under the "products" category (see the previous section, "The Two Sides of Tech Marketing"). Companies that hire "MarCom Managers" are typically either very small and are looking to hire marketing generalists, or are simply signifying that they are looking for someone with strong writing, editing or design skills as opposed to product or market expertise. The term "MarCom Manager" is used differently by so many companies that it is impossible to try to classify it in detail. To make things even more confusing, some companies call MarCom "Corporate Communications," which is very different from the specialized CorpComm role described in Chapter 11.

- **Services Marketing Managers** *are* Product Marketing Managers, but the "product" is one or more service offerings.

- **Strategic Marketing** is an area that has absolutely no standardized definition. This tends to be a catch-all title for roles combining aspects of Product Marketing, Market Development, Competitive Analysis and more. For instance, a Strategic Marketer might work with the Finance department to evaluate foreign markets that the company might consider entering.

- **Marketing Research** typically involves a mix of qualitative (for instance, focus groups) and quantitative (surveys) data collection methods from prospective customers to assess their interest in a new product or service. Most tech companies do this, whether formally or informally, but it is usually performed either as one of many duties held by a marketing manager (usually Product Marketing or Product Management), or at least mostly outsourced to a firm that specializes in market research. Only a small number of tech companies have dedicated Marketing Researchers on staff.

- **Brand Marketing** is a somewhat nebulous interdisciplinary field that focuses on defining and upholding a company's or product's brand image or reputation. It may involve working with Product Marketers, Corporate Communications, Product Design, and outside PR and advertising agencies. This position is generally only found in very large tech companies.

CHAPTER THREE

Product Marketing and Product Management

Product Marketing Managers (PMMs) and Product Managers (PMs) are similar roles but with key differences between them. Because it is easiest to explain those differences by contrasting them side-by-side, both roles are explored in this chapter.

Both roles are somewhat unique within companies in that they simultaneously involve the dichotomy mentioned in the introductory marketing chapter of being both a voice for the company and a voice for the customer.

Instead of Marketing, the Product Management function may be a part of the Engineering department or even be a standalone department. In any case, PMs work closely with Marketing and it is useful to understand their role.

What They Do

Product Marketing Managers (more commonly just called Product Marketers) generally perform three broad sets of activities. The first set, which all PMMs do, is write and continuously update product-focused marketing collateral. This includes documents such as technical data sheets, brochures, white papers, website copy and sales presentations. These materials serve, in part, as the "voice of the company" to the market. Note that the kinds of materials PMs create are different than those that MarCom groups (see Chapter 2 for more about MarCom) create. MarCom generally focuses on positioning the company and on establishing a brand, and the audience for those materials includes prospective customers but also the general public, the media, and industry analysts. Product marketers only focus on the products, and the target audience is prospective customers. The goal of these materials is to explain what the products do and what benefits they offer to customers.

The second broad role PMMs play is developing product positioning. Product positioning is a somewhat amorphous concept, but essentially it involves defining a set of key points or statements that help everyone in the company appropriately articulate the most important product attributes for a given audience. As an example, if a Partner Marketing Manager is taking to a partner about an upcoming product release, what specifically should he or she say about that product? Or, if a Public Relations Manager is speaking to a reporter about a new product, what key points should he or she emphasize to ensure that the company gets accurate, favorable product coverage?

The third and perhaps most important function *most* product marketers perform is gathering market requirements from current and prospective customers, and feeding that information to the Product Management and/or Engineering teams to ensure that the right products – products that the market truly wants – are developed. This is the "voice of the customer" component.

Product marketers collect this information from a variety of sources, ranging from interviewing prospective customers and industry experts, to conducting surveys, monitoring competitors' actions and many other techniques. Product marketers capture these requirements in what's called an MRD (Market Requirements Document). In most companies, the MRDs are then reviewed by Product Managers, who adapt these higher-level, non-product-specific market requirements in the MRD into a PRD (a Product Requirements Document). An MRD defines what the market needs in terms of product capabilities, while the PRD defines in technical terms what the company needs to build to fulfill those market needs. Product Managers typically negotiate with Engineering departments to determine what features will or won't be included, and on what timeline, using the PRD as a reference and the MRD more for context.

In some companies, this third function – inbound market requirements gathering – is performed entirely by Product Managers, in which case Product Marketers typically focus on creating marketing collateral. And in extremely sales-driven companies, decisions about what products to build are made entirely by some combination of Sales management, Engineering managers, and the executive leadership of the company.

In addition to these broad functions, Product Marketers often perform a wide array of other roles. These exact same roles may be performed by Product Managers, instead. The most common roles include:

- *Competitive intelligence* is discussed in much more detail in Chapter 8, but essentially it entails tracking what the company's competitors are doing, and using that information to help Sales sell against competitors' advantages or helping the company decide if it should build or modify products to compete more effectively.

- *Sales training* involves educating the Sales team on how to position newly introduced product features, how to sell against competitors' features, and at a higher level how to understand the market for the product.
- *Product pricing* is usually developed jointly between Marketing managers, Sales managers and the Finance department. Even so, the PMM usually maintains the official price list.
- *Market evangelism* is a fancy way to express that most PMMs and PMs conduct seminars and webinars (a seminar delivered over the Internet) and speak at industry events of all kinds.

Useful Skills

PMs and PMMs need a broad range of skills. These include:

Technical skills. Product Marketing and Product Management are the most technical roles in Marketing organizations. It is thus necessary for PMs and PMMs to have a solid grounding in the technologies their companies build. PMMs don't necessarily need a technical undergraduate degree – in fact, most don't have one – but they should at least have some hands-on technical skill. At a minimum, for example, a PMM in a Web software firm should know how to write HTML script. Get your feet wet. If you'd like to work for a computer hardware manufacturer, try building a PC at home. If you want to work for an Internet service provider, build a website. If necessary, take as many technical computer-related courses as you can.

Because PMs typically interface with Engineering departments, most PMs do have a technical undergraduate degree or more hands-on experience (self-taught computer programmers, for instance).

Most importantly, PMs and PMMs need to *like* technology, and need to be willing to keep learning about new products and technologies. If obsessing over product features, benefits and technical specifications sounds boring, this isn't the right field for you.

Interpersonal skills. PMs and PMMs work with a lot of people, both internally and externally. Internally, they work with virtually every department in the company (PMs work more with Engineering, while PMMs work more with Sales and other Marketing functions). A certain level of diplomacy is thus very helpful. In addition, PMs and PMMs hold customer-facing roles. As such, they should have polished interpersonal skills. They should be comfortable meeting new people.

Communications skills. PMs and PMMs need to be effective communicators, on many fronts. First, almost all PMs and PMMs speak in public, whether presenting a seminar, delivering a webinar, or meeting with a group of customers. To be successful, you need to be comfortable speaking in public. If you fear speaking in public, join your local Toastmasters club or read books on conquering a fear of public speaking.

Second, both roles require writing skill. PMs tend to write documents such as PRDs only for internal consumption, so writing skill is perhaps slightly less important. But PMMs need to be particularly good writers, as they are writing a variety of documents that will be visible to potentially thousands of readers. (Of course, most tech firms either have MarCom staff onboard who are good editors or they outsource editing to freelance contractors, but still, being a strong writer as a PMM goes a long way.)

Business skills. Good PMs and PMMs understand more than products – they understand business. Many PMs and PMMs hold MBAs, and increasingly employers prefer candidates who have one.

Sales and marketing skills. Even though PMs and PMMs are more technically focused than other marketing professionals in a tech firm, they are, first and foremost, marketers. If you have an undergraduate degree in Marketing, you might be fine in this regard. If not, take an introductory marketing course to familiarize yourself with the jargon that all marketers use. Longer-term, consider pursuing an MBA, whether full- or part-time.

Another invaluable skill is being able to think like a salesperson. If you have some solid Sales experience (sorry, working retail in high school doesn't count), you're already ahead of most other candidates.

PM/PMM process skills. Finally, whether you're interested in product marketing or management, I *strongly* recommend you take attend a Pragmatic Marketing seminar (pragmaticmarketing.com). If you're serious about pursuing a career as a PM or PMM, these courses are invaluable.

Career Paths

PMs and PMMs start their careers with that title at the Manager or Specialist level; I have never run into a PM or PMM with a title lower than that, though it probably happens. Managers generally focus on one or more product lines, class of products, or a particular market segment (see Chapter 6). Directors typically lead a team of PMs or PMMs.

The VPs of Marketing at many tech firms moved up through a PM or PMM track. The combination of product and market knowledge, direct exposure to customers, and the opportunity to work with multiple departments internally provides a very strong foundation for leadership success.

CHAPTER FOUR

Field Marketing

F ield is just another term for "the Sales team." More commonly, it refers specifically to the salespeople who are based in remote or home offices away from the company's headquarters, though this distinction is by no means universal. A Field Marketer may be assigned to work exclusively with one or more salespeople, or can be assigned a particular territory (geographic region). Smaller companies may only have one Field Marketer who supports the entire sales force.

Field Marketers have a simple mission: support the Sales team with whatever it needs to win deals. This role is also sometimes called Field Enablement or Sales Enablement, because individuals in this position "enable" the Sales team to sell more effectively. The form of that support could be just about anything, but usually involves some amount of customized documentation or marketing collateral. For instance, a Sales Executive may feel that a particular customer would like to see a sales presentation that is better tailored to their specific needs than the standard corporate sales presentation. Or, perhaps the Sales Executive feels that a comparative analysis of the return on investment (ROI) that similar customers experience by using the company's products would help seal the deal.

The work that Field Marketers and Product Marketers do is similar, but there are some important differences. While both Field

Marketers and Product Marketers create collateral and sales tools, the focus is usually different. Field Marketers are strapped to the hip with salespeople and do a lot of "one-off" work. That is, the materials created by a Field Marketer are usually specific to one customer or type of customer, and may not be reusable to help close other deals. In contrast, Product Marketers generally focus on creating materials that would be of interest to the largest possible customer base, though not necessarily specific to any of them.

There are some other important differences between Field and Product Marketing. Field Marketers don't perform the side of Product Marketing that involves collecting customer and market requirements and working with Product Managers and Engineering to transform those requirements into new or modified products. In addition, Field Marketers aren't as concerned with creating the most elegant deliverable so much as creating the one that they can create or modify quickly to help win only whatever deal cycle they are currently involved in (and at the highest price). Finally, Field Marketers don't work on materials or projects that have no direct linkage to driving sales. For example, Product Marketers occasionally work on projects with MarCom and CorpComm groups that don't directly drive sales. But if it doesn't directly effect sales, Field Marketers aren't interested.

You may be wondering why Field Marketers are in Marketing organizations and not in Sales. Well, in some companies they are – though they hold different job titles which de-emphasize the marketing terminology. Even so, whatever companies call these individuals, the deliverables Field Marketers produce are traditional marketing pieces. And the skills that good Field Marketers possess are generally the same skills that other good marketing profession-als possess.

What They Do

Field Marketers are highly output-driven. They produce the same kinds of materials that Product Marketers produce, but again the focus is on taking whatever collateral already exists and tailoring it to fit the needs of the sales cycle they are supporting, or to create something new from scratch, though it will probably be a one-off. The deliverables Field Marketers produce is dictated by what Sales tells them they need, which in turn is dictated by what prospective customers ask for above and beyond whatever "off the shelf" mar-keting materials are already available.

Here's a common scenario: A company has dozens of case stu-dies of customer successes, all summarized in one long white pa-per. But a prospective customer can only relate to a handful of those case studies (because it covers different industries) and isn't im-pressed by the others. The Sales Executive suspects that if the pros-pect received a more tailored case study document to show to its Board of Directors, the prospect would purchase the company's software. The Sales Executive asks the Field Marketer to alter the documentation by stripping out the non-relevant case studies, ela-borate on the ones of interest, and re-package the document in a more "digestable" format for distribution at the next Board meet-ing.

The kinds of assistance that Field Marketers provide runs the gamut. It can range from wordsmithing an email about to go out to a prospect, to coaching a salesperson on how to deliver a particular sales presentation more effectively, to creating a 10-page document to help the staff at the prospective customer understand how the company's products will uniquely benefit them, specifically.

Field Marketers may also be involved in projects to boost the productivity of the Sales team. For instance, they may implement a new automated proposal generation software tool, build pricing calculators for complex sales quotes, design and conduct sales training sessions, or design and manage an Intranet site (sometimes called a "sales portal") for organizing and disseminating information and materials to the Sales team. By facilitating such projects, the Field Marketer attempts to make *every* salesperson more effective on *every* deal.

Some Field Marketers also work on lead generation programs, and at some tech companies lead generation is one of the primary roles of a Field Marketer. This function is covered in the section on Marketing Programs Management

Finally, Field Marketers may work closely with someone in Competitive Analysis, Product Marketing, or Product Management to conduct "win/loss analyses" – delving deep into why the company won or lost deals against key competitors.

Useful Skills

Since Field Marketers work side-by-side with salespeople, having a strong understanding of sales processes is mandatory. Perhaps more importantly, you should know how salespeople think. This doesn't require that you have been a salesperson, but it would certainly help.

As with most Marketing roles, strong writing skills are exceptionally useful – in particular, the ability to write in a concise, business-oriented style. It also helps to be adept at conveying information in graphical formats (charts, graphs, tables, etc.), because in difficult sales cycles a picture really can say (and save) a thousand words.

Strong presentation skills are also key. Field Marketers often find themselves in customer-facing situations, whether face-to-face in a sales call meeting or on a phone call.

Career Paths

Field Marketing tends to be a mid-level position, and most Field Marketers hold the title of "Manager." Directors and VPs of Field Marketing are only common in the largest tech companies.

Most Field Marketers enter the role with a few years of experience in another Marketing field (especially Product Marketing or Management), in Sales, or in Sales Engineering. The transition can work the other way, too; Field Marketing is an excellent preparatory role for those same roles.

CHAPTER FIVE

Market Development

Market Developers, simply put, help companies enter new markets. The term "market" may refer to an industry (a "vertical") the company previously hadn't sold to, a new type of product, or a new geographic region. You will sometimes see words like "Emerging" prefixed to the title of "Market Development Manager" to stress the focus on *new* products or markets.

Market Developers aren't used every time a company enters any new market, but rather only when some dedicated marketing attention is needed. For example, Convio successfully sold software to every type ("segment") of nonprofit organization except one: hospital foundations. As this represented a large potential market for Convio, and because the strategies and tactics required to sell to hospital foundations were different from, say, selling to a humane society, it made sense to put a dedicated Market Developer (yours truly) on the hospital segment.

As another example, since its inception Lombardi's software ran locally on personal computers. But in 2007, Lombardi decided to launch a new Web-based version of its software which customers would access over the Internet. As this represented an entirely new product line for Lombardi and necessitated different marketing strategies and tactics to succeed, they hired a Director of Market Development for this product line.

What They Do

What a Market Developer does depends on when he or she takes on the role. Market Developers can be brought in while a company is in the process of determining whether to enter a market, or which one. In this case, the individual would initially focus on researching and analyzing the market opportunity. Market Developers can also be brought in after some progress has already been made in tackling a market, in which case the Market Developer will be more focused on refining and executing a marketing plan instead of defining one from scratch.

Market Development is a blend of strategic and tactical work. On the strategic side are research, analysis and planning. On the tactical side are activities such as sales support and executing marketing campaigns. The types of work Market Developers may perform include:

- *Researching market opportunities.* Which markets are desirable for the company to pursue? What characteristics of those markets are complementary to the company's strategy and past success?

- *Building business cases.* Of the desirable markets, which ones could generate the most revenue for the company? Why is this market better than others the company could pursue? What resources (such as money, people, and time) are required to enter this market? Business cases that require significant investment might require approval by a company's executive team or Board of Directors.

- *Market segmentation.* How can the market be categorized or sub-categorized (segmented)? Are there desirable niche markets within the broader market category? For example, "hospital foundations" could be segmented into children's hospital foundations, cancer center foundations, and so on.

- *Marketing plan development.* With desirable markets and sub-segments identified, how should the company approach this market from a marketing perspective? To build awareness in a new market, should the company launch an advertising campaign, exhibit at trade shows, use direct mail or telemarketing to reach potential customers, or conduct free seminars or webinars, or employ other tactics? What should the high-level messages of these campaigns be? How will success be measured? What will the marketing campaigns cost?

- *Product input.* What product changes or new products, if any, are required to meet the unique needs of this market? Market Developers frequently work with Product Marketers and Product Managers to define new or enhanced functionality requirements.

- *Sales support.* Entering new markets usually requires that the Sales team be trained on how to sell to this market. New sales tools, new pricing models, and new marketing collateral might be required. Certain sales channel partners might need to tapped, as well.

- *Tracking progress.* Market Developers typically establish a "dashboard" of quantifiable metrics (sometimes called KSIs, or Key Success Indicators) to track the success of their efforts. These may include sales leads generated, number of new customers, revenue, marketing expenses, media coverage, end users, and many other metrics. Beyond defining and setting up systems to track these metrics, a critical facet of market development is continually monitoring these indicators, analyzing what's causing changes in the metrics over time, adjusting marketing strategies to improve them, and altering forecasts accordingly. It's also critical for a Market Developer to be able to use these metrics to justify continued investment in the market.

Useful Skills

Market Development requires a broad range of skills, most of which are best obtained through several years of work experience, especially in interdisciplinary roles. These include:

- *Balance.* As mentioned earlier, Market Development requires a blend of strategic thinking and tactical execution. You need to be good at both.

- *Analytical skills.* Market Developers need to be strong at analyzing data, trends and other information to determine the relative attractiveness of market opportunities, as well as predict potential obstacles to market success.

- *Financial skills*. Market Developers should have at least basic financial skills to be able to calculate projected revenues and costs for pursuing various market-entry strategies. You should be adept at using Microsoft Excel.

- *Market knowledge*. Having expert familiarity with the market you'll be developing is always a plus but rarely mandatory. Much more important is the ability to learn about new markets quickly by asking the right questions, and focusing on the most relevant issues. In fact, in some cases, already having in-depth market knowledge may be detrimental because it can cloud objectivity.

- *Familiarity with the company*. To determine the viability of a particular company entering a new market, it helps to know a lot about the company and what has or hasn't worked in the past. Markets that look attractive on paper may be completely wrong for the company's Sales team to pursue, for the company's culture, or for the company's market reputation. Good Market Developers take these "fit" issues into account as best they can, but when defining which market to enter or how to do it, it helps to know enough about the company from experience to be able to make faster, better informed "reality check" decisions about such things. This is why many Market Developers start their careers in another function in the company and move into Market Development only when they've amassed a significant amount of knowledge and experience.

- *Interpersonal skills.* One hard part about market development is keeping executives in your company behind your efforts. Despite your best efforts, new markets may be painfully slow to develop, and as a Market Developer you may find yourself continually fighting for scarce resources to keep your marketing efforts funded. Being able to keep the executive team excited and committed to the market – and committed to supporting you, personally – is critical.

Career Paths

Any road can lead you into market development. Most Market Developers fall into it unintentionally, often coming from backgrounds in another Marketing or Sales role, or from a background that is heavy in analysis, such as management consulting or finance.

Market Development is rarely an entry-level position. It's usually not a good field to enter without at least five years of professional work experience, or fewer years but with some refined analytical or financial training. Many Market Developers hold MBAs.

In smaller- to mid-sized companies, Market Development staff typically report up to the Vice President of Marketing, either directly or through a Director of Market Development. Larger companies may have a dedicated VP of Market Development.

Market Development is an excellent springboard to advancement within a company, and to other careers. If a Market Developer does a particularly good job of developing a new market that grows large enough to justify dedicated management, many companies will tap the individual to run a new business unit focused on that market or, in a smaller company, make him or her the Segment Marketer for that segment. In some companies, Market Developers focus on one market only until it gains substantial traction and then move on to develop another market. Other Market Developers move into Sales roles to sell into the new market.

CHAPTER SIX

Segment Marketing

Segment Marketers – also called Vertical or Industry Marketers – take over where Market Developers leave off. As explained in the previous chapter, the principle function of Market Developers is to spearhead a company's charge into a new or relatively untapped market segment. Once the Market Developer has helped the company gain some initial traction in that new segment, someone with a slightly different skillset is often called upon to maintain that traction. Market Developers get the ball rolling, and Segment Marketers keep it rolling.

A "segment" usually means an industry (for example, computer equipment manufacturers), a sub-segment thereof (for example, computer printer manufacturers), or a new geographic region. However, "segment" can also mean a product or line of products, or a combination of verticals, territories, and product lines. Some tech firms segment by size of customer. More generally, a segment is just a niche, and there are no bounds on how granular these niches can be. A segment could be, for example, consumers in a particular age range who live in Iowa.

Dell Computer, for instance, markets to four segments: home and home office users, small business customers, medium and large business customers, and government, education and healthcare customers. For each of these segments, Dell offers different products and services, at different prices, and packaged in different bundles.

And the marketing tactics employed to reach and appeal to these four segments is different; for example, large business customers may have dedicated Account Executive, while consumers do not. These kinds of marketing issues that vary by segment are defined and managed by Segment Marketers.

Segment Marketers are a cross between a Product Marketer and a Field Marketer. In fact, the work individuals in these three roles perform may overlap. You can think of the Segment Marketer's job as a subset of what a Product Marketer does. Product Marketers typically own "horizontals" – one or more products or product lines that can be sold to customers in one or more verticals (industries). In contrast, Segment Marketers typically only care about the vertical. If certain products aren't well suited to their vertical, Segment Marketers aren't concerned about those products. Likewise, Segment Marketers are only concerned about the specific capabilities of those products that are valued by customers in the segment(s) they manage.

What They Do

Segment marketing is both a tactical and a strategic role. It's tactical in the sense that, just like product marketing, segment marketing requires the creation of collateral and sales tools. A Segment Marketer may, in fact, do absolutely everything a Product Marketer at the same company does, except that the deliverables produced will be specific to one or more segments and will typically de-emphasize the more technical product capabilities in favor of more benefit-focused collateral tailored to the unique interests of the segment.

On another tactical front, Segment Marketers typically define and implement a wide array of marketing campaigns to grow their segment. The scope of these campaigns ranges from generating awareness to generating sales leads. Segment Marketers will thus often work closely with Marketing Program Managers.

Nobody knows a company's market segments like the Segment Marketers in charge of them. Segment marketing can therefore be highly strategic, on three fronts. First, Segment Marketers often need to define and continuously refine the marketing tactics they use in their segment. The tactics used by a Market Developer to "seed" the market may have been appropriate to gain initial traction in a segment, but those might no longer be appropriate a few months later.

Segment Marketing can also be highly strategic in companies such as Microsoft where Segment Marketers play the role of a customer advocate in a given industry sector. Segment Marketers are often one of "the voices of the customer" in internal discussions about product strategy and corporate vision. Their insight and feedback to internal groups is invaluable.

Third, Segment Marketers typically become "domain experts" about the dynamics of their segment – including what unique strengths and weaknesses competitors have. Their knowledge thus provides valuable strategic feedback to others in the company, such as Competitive Analysts and Product Managers.

Career Paths
The same backgrounds and skills that are good for Product and Field Marketers apply to Segment Marketers. Many marketing pro-

fessionals move easily between these three roles (or come from a background in market development). The obvious caveat here is that it's helpful for a Segment Marketer to have some domain knowledge about the segment on which he or she will be focused. Lacking that domain knowledge, it's critical that the Segment Marketer be a quick learner and be comfortable doing the research to learn about the unique needs of the segment.

CHAPTER SEVEN

Partner, Channel and Alliance Marketing

Partner Marketers are the Marketing liaison between a company and its partners. For a tech company, "partners" usually include some combination of:

- **Sales channel partners** – Organizations that sell the company's products, either under the company's brand name or their own, "private label" versions. (Partner Marketers who focus entirely on sales channel partnerships are usually referred to as Channel Marketing Managers.)
- **Technology partners** – Also called "solutions partners," these are typically hardware or software vendors that make products complementary to the company's. For instance, electronic health record (EHR) software runs on tablet computers, and the two are usually sold together. Most EHR vendors thus have formal partnerships with certain computer manufacturers.
- **Service partners** – Third-party vendors that deploy, administer, service or support the company's products.
- **Solutions partners** – An inconsistently used term that usually means some combination of the three partner types above.
- **Consultants** – Some tech companies tap the influence of consultants of various kinds to help promote their products and services.

- **Professional Associations** – Most tech companies and their customers belong to or are otherwise involved in one or more associations of various kinds.

Once a company forms a significant number of partnerships – or when the strategic importance of even a small number of partnerships reaches a critical threshold of unmanageability – most companies hire people to manage those relationships. The overall business relationship may be managed by one or more functions within the company. For example, Sales may "own" relationships with sales channel partners, and Engineering may own relationships with technology partners. However, most of these relationships will involve some joint marketing activities. This is where Partner Marketers come in.

What They Do

Partners may work with companies on a variety of joint marketing fronts. For instance:

- Press releases announcing the formation of a partnership or milestones reached, such as successful new product integration or joint new customer wins.
- Joint exhibition at industry trade shows or other events.
- Joint speaking opportunities, whether at conferences or in seminars and webinars.
- Development of co-authored white papers, research studies, or case studies.

- Joint advertising or other forms of co-promotion, such as co-sponsorship of a conference.
- Conferences especially for partners.
- Formation and ongoing management of partner advisory boards.

In most cases the Partner Marketer doesn't single-handedly develop or create all of these things, though he or she is ultimately responsible for making sure it gets done. For example, most of a joint press release would be written by PR Managers, and much of the logistical work involved in planning a joint event would be handled by, for example, an Events Coordinator. But the Partner Marketer would bear overall responsibility for the projects and would play an active role in planning and coordinating joint marketing strategies and activities. For instance, while a PR Manager may actually write the press release, the Partner Marketer would work with the partner to jointly define the high-level messaging that the press release should encapsulate.

Beyond the execution of joint marketing activities, Partner Marketers typically establish, support and enforce mutually agreed upon goals for the partnerships. These can range from somewhat vague objectives such as "work together to promote our alliance" to concrete, quantifiable goals such as "drive $10 million in new business to each other's company by 2010." Such goals are often rolled-up into a broader annual or quarterly co-marketing plan, which Partner Marketers at both companies jointly establish.

Is This the Same Thing as Business Development?

Business Development is one of the most inconsistently defined positions in the tech sector. It's similar to Partner Marketing but has a different focus. First, some quick history: in the 1990s, tiny tech companies attempted to make themselves *seem* much bigger by forming partnerships with as many companies as they could. Most of these partnerships constituted nothing more than joint marketing activities with no clear purpose in mind. For instance, at one point, *every* tech company seemed to be partners with tech titans like IBM, even if all that meant was they use IBM computers in their office. The individuals who drove these partnerships were called Business Developers, which was often shortened to "biz dev" or just "BD."

Over time, tech companies progressively de-emphasized focusing on touchy-feely partnerships that produced no tangible benefits to either party. Instead, BD teams now focus on partnerships that directly or indirectly generate revenue for their company, either from product sales or services such as deployment or product customization. For instance, BD will strike partnerships that give a "finder's fee" (a sales commission) to third parties that refer new business to them. Likewise, the partner may pay the company for any professional services work that the company sends their way.

Most BD partnerships involve some level of joint marketing, too. But the difference between a traditional Partner Marketer and a Business Developer is that BD is *primarily* concerned with cultivating and managing revenue-enhancing partnerships, while Partner Marketers are *primarily* concerned with managing joint marketing activities, even for partnerships that have no revenue-generating component. Some tech companies have separate BD and Partner Marketing functions, while at other companies these roles are blended together and may be called *either* Business Development or Partner Marketing.

Partner Marketers may also develop special marketing collateral, sales and training tools, partner extranets, partner recruitment programs, and other materials and programs to attract and support partners. Some Partner Marketers, for instance, develop a "welcome kit" of materials for new partners, and develop branding guides to ensure that partners use your company's logo, name, and other graphical and text elements correctly.

Some Partner Marketers are also charged with identifying and recruiting partners to fill strategic "holes." For example, a company's product may need a new feature to reach a critical market segment. Developing that feature internally may be time and labor intensive, which will greatly delay the company in selling to that segment, and they may lose the opportunity to a faster competitor. In conjunction with a Product Manager or Engineer, the Partner Marketer could seek out a technology partnership with another company that can provide the missing feature.

As another example, a company may need to reach a new market tier. If they currently sell into top market tiers (very large companies), and top-tier sales growth slows or stops, they may turn to the mid-sized company market (the "mid-market") for growth opportunities. Having no mid-market sales experience in their own sales organization, the Partner Marketer could reach out to resellers and other sales channels that specialize in selling to the mid-market.

Managing ongoing communications with partners is a critical role. Partners need to be continuously "kept in the loop" about what your company is doing, especially regarding new product introductions, shifts in corporate strategy, upcoming marketing pushes, and recent sales wins.

Partner Marketers who manage Technology and Service partners may also work internally with Product Managers and Product Marketers to modify existing products or shape future product directions to accommodate the partners' needs. For example, a software deployment partner may request the company build-in tools to help accelerate the deployment process. In such a scenario, the Partner Marketer may represent the "voice of the partner" to internal Product Management and Engineering teams.

Another area in which some Partner Marketers get involved is in partner certification. This usually applies only to Technology or Service partners, but variants may exist for any kind of partner. A certification is a credential that a partner has met whatever steps are necessary to become an "official" partner of the company. This typically means the partner has been trained on integrating with or deploying the product, or has been through a sales training program. A Partner Marketer may define the certification process, actively recruit partners to go through it, specify rules about the partner's use of the term "certified" in their own promotional efforts, and much more, depending on the needs of the company.

Finally, Partner Marketers are usually active involved in marketing the partner program itself. Prospective partners and prospective customers need to know who your company works with, and what benefits can be delivered jointly by your company and those partners. Sometimes the answer is obvious, but at other times it is more subtle.

Useful Skills

Simply put, you must be good with people. Partner Marketing is an externally facing role. Your company will expect you to always maintain a high degree or professionalism to put a good face on the company. This can be exceedingly difficult at times, as the partners you work with may have competing marketing priorities, time-tables, and resources. This can be a frustrating job, so excellent interpersonal skills and a healthy dose of patience will prove invaluable.

Project management skills are also critical. You may be juggling multiple projects with partners at any one time. Being able to keep projects on time and within budget without letting anything slip through the cracks is critical. This is a great role for people who pay incredible attention to the details.

Good Partner Marketers are creative. Some joint marketing plans inevitably go haywire. For instance, due to a slump in sales a partner may abruptly cancel their co-sponsorship of an event your company is putting on. Finding a way out of such situations will require some creativity and problem-solving skills. Patience again comes into play here.

The ability to work with a team is of course also invaluable. As mentioned earlier, Partner Marketers typically rely on others internally to execute many of the deliverables they define with partners. The ability to persuade and motivate others within your company to "get it done" for you is key.

Partner Marketers might be involved in executing legal contracts with partners to commit to specific goals (usually around re-selling the company's products). If so, specific expertise in contract negotiation may be necessary.

To manage sales channel partnerships, specifically, a basic understanding of how sales channels work is essential. Sales channels for hardware companies can be particularly complex, involving distributors, resellers, systems integrators, and other parties.

Career Paths

The extent to which Partner Marketing is more of a junior versus a senior role depends on the strategic importance of partners to the company. In companies where partners are few in number or not strategically critical, Partner Marketing is often undertaken by less experienced individuals. In that case, Partner Marketing may be an excellent first job in a tech company. In larger tech companies, where partnerships may be vast in number or scope, seasoned marketing professionals with over ten years of overall work experience are generally sought. Most Partner Marketing roles fall somewhere in between.

Those with backgrounds in managing relationships with customers – Account Managers, Customer Service professionals, most Sales roles, etc. – are particularly well-suited to a position in Partner Marketing. Individuals with experience in managing events or those with a general, interdisciplinary marketing background are also strong candidates.

Managing certain *types* of partners may require or benefit from specific skills or experience. For example, managing joint marketing activities with foreign-based partners may necessitate that you possess foreign language skills and have a high degree of cultural sensitivity, and that you are comfortable working with international PR firms.

CHAPTER EIGHT

Competitive Analysis/Intelligence

As in any industry, every tech company has competitors. But tech companies have a particular challenge with competition in that the barriers to competing with a tech company are often dangerously low. It is relatively easy, for example, to build a nearly exact copy of another company's website, or to tear down and reverse-engineer a hardware product to figure out what makes it tick and then build a new product very similar to it – or better.

In addition, tech companies, all the employees who work for those companies, and all the people who buy their products and services are meshed in a tangled web of information exchange, all enabled by the Internet. More so than in most industries, there are few secrets in tech.

How, then, do tech companies survive against each other? One way is to "execute better" – even if your competitor makes a product better than yours, if your company can *sell* it better, your company will win in the market. The other way is to predict what your competitors will do, analyze what they are doing or have done, tailor your marketing messages to position your company better versus them, and train your Sales team how to attack your competitors' weaknesses. This is the art of competitive analysis.

In smaller tech companies, competitive analysis is usually managed by Product Marketing or Product Management. As a tech company grows, or as its market becomes more competitive (because there are more competitors, or because the competitors have gotten "smarter"), the need for a dedicated Competitive Analyst becomes apparent.

What They Do

A Competitive Analyst is a cross between a researcher, a detective, and strategist. At the highest level, they gather information, analyze it, and disseminate findings and recommendations. There are a lot of sub-steps in that process.

First, Competitive Analysts have to stay on top of what their competitors are doing. At a minimum, this involves reading competitors' press releases and any media coverage about them, monitoring their websites for updated product information, and tracking what trade shows or other industry events they attend and evaluating what they do there.

Beyond that, a Competitive Analyst needs to establish a programmatic way to collect intelligence from the richest source: the Sales team. Salespeople and Sales Engineers are constantly exposed to valuable competitive insights while engaged in a sales cycle. A prospect may tell them, for example, that Competitor X underbid your company's price by 15%, or that Competitor Y has a new product coming out in three months that will render your comparable product obsolete. A good Competitive Analyst will train the Sales team to report any and all such nuggets of information to him, whether in person, by email, by phone, or perhaps by a form on the company intranet.

The second part of competitive analysis is analyzing all the information collected. This is done on an ongoing basis. The Analyst needs to sift through all intelligence collected recently as well as all historical intelligence and discern what is important and what is credible, with an eye for trends and patterns. For instance, if a competitor underbids you by 15% just once when they typically bid about the same price, that may be a fluke. But what if they've done that consistently in the last five deals? Or what if they've done that repeatedly, but only in deals in a particular territory, or when selling to customers in a particular vertical, or for a specific product? Perhaps an ambitious new salesperson is trying to win more deals in his territory; perhaps the competitor wants to increase its market share in a particular vertical (which may signal that they have a Market Developer or Segment Marketer assigned to it); or maybe the competitor is about to discontinue a hardware product line and is selling its remaining inventory at a blowout price.

Like a scientist, a Competitive Analyst needs to formulate a hypothesis about what's happening and seek support for it by evaluating all the intelligence he has collected. Once he believes he knows what a competitor is up to, the Analyst needs to disseminate the information.

The primary audience for what a Competitive Analyst discovers is usually Sales and Product Management. The Sales team is of course interested in how to combat competitors more effectively. Sometimes all the Analyst needs to do is give Sales a "heads-up" about what competitors are doing, such as making a new claim in sales cycles, using a new pricing model, or launching a new product. In other cases, complex new developments may require training the Sales team more formally, perhaps at a quarterly sales training session.

Salespeople also tend to like "killpoints" and "traps." Killpoints are simple but effective arguments and counter-claims to shoot down detrimental claims made by competitors about your company in deal cycles. For instance, a competitor may have discovered a bug in your software and is telling your prospective customers about it. Your Sales team needs to know precisely what to say in response when your prospect asks about it. Traps or "landmines" are essentially killpoints made ahead of time. Before a prospective customer asks about that software bug, what can a salesperson say that would make the competitor look bad if they brought it up?

The other primary beneficiary of competitive analysis is Product Management, which is interested in knowing what features competitors' products have and how those products work. This includes more subtle product characteristics as "look and feel" or overall ease of use. Product Managers use this information to ensure that they're building the right products to compete effectively.

Other groups in the company may be interested, too. Market Developers and Segment Marketers would find it useful to know how competitors are tackling the markets they're focused on. Certain partners may find such information useful, too. And all Executives, especially in a public company, need to be prepared to answer questions from investors and the media about their competition.

If you think this all sounds like what the Central Intelligence Agency does, you're right. The "intelligence game" – whether it's about companies or governments – is played essentially the same way.

Useful Skills

There is an art and a science to competitive analysis. Most important is to be a strategic thinker. The hardest part of CI is not understanding what a competitor already did but rather *predicting* what they might do, proactively assessing what impact that might have, and planning for the worst. This takes imagination and creativity.

It also helps to be able to spot broader historical and current trends and think several steps ahead. Good chess players have this skill.

Finally, understanding the sales process and, in particular, how salespeople work is essential. Unless the Analyst can translate his or her findings into usable and effective anti-competitive tactics, the information and analysis is by itself worthless. The insight of what to give Sales to help them do their jobs better takes time and patience to acquire.

Career Paths

There's no common background for competitive analysis. Most people tend to fall into it from Product Marketing or Product Management roles, where it's often one of their many job responsibilities (especially in smaller tech companies).

CI is rarely an entry-level job. To do it well generally requires a diverse range of experience in marketing or sales, and many employers now seek Analysts who hold an MBA. Even so, some companies hire less experienced analysts at the Associate level to perform some of the more tactical components of CI, such as monitoring the media for valuable insights.

Knowing your market – the competitors, the customers' needs, and what's changing in the industries your company serves – is critical. This is why many Analysts are hired into tech companies from companies in the target markets they serve.

Strong analytical skills are also important. This is one reason many tech companies seek those with a Master's degree (MBA, MS in Marketing Research, or similar), or work experience with a large consulting firm with an "analysis heavy" focus.

If you're interested in the CI field, you may want to join the Society of Competitive Intelligence Professionals (SCIP; see www.scip.org).

CHAPTER NINE

Marketing Programs Management

Marketing programs – also called campaigns – are activities that help build awareness in the market about a company's products and services and in turn ultimately generate leads from prospective customers. These activities typically include some combination of direct mail, telemarketing, email marketing, webcasts (or "webinars"), events, and online advertising. Marketing Programs involve planning, executing, evaluating, and refining these activities.

Marketing campaigns are typically run for one of two reasons: leads or awareness. These goals are distinct but related. The goal of a lead generation (more commonly called "lead gen," or sometimes "demand gen") campaign is to acquire contact information for prospective customers. To get this information, some kind of compelling, trackable incentive or "call to action" is usually made. For example, "provide your contact information through this online form to receive a free copy of a useful whitepaper," or "drop off your business card at our trade show booth to be entered into a drawing to win a free iPod."

The second type of campaign is to generate awareness about the company (especially if the company was recently formed or is in an unusually competitive market where it's hard to stand out) or perhaps about a new product. An awareness-focused campaign doesn't necessarily have a desired action attached to it, or at least not in the short-term. Think about an advertisement you might see in a magazine or on a billboard; even if you're not in the market for the advertiser's product right now, the hope is that by seeing the ad the product will remain "top of mind" for you and you'll remember it when you're in the market for such a product in the future. Or consider the case of a tech company exhibiting at a trade show. Even if prospective customers don't come to your company's booth, there may be value in simply "being seen" there because passers-by may recall your company at a later time. Lead gen and awareness are linked, because awareness of a company and its products primes prospective customers to be interested in doing business with your company. Note that marketing programs at some tech companies involve only lead generation campaigns and leave all awareness-building activities to MarCom or outside agencies.

There are two broad sides to marketing programs: planning and execution. In a small company, one person may handle both. Larger companies typically have two or more people to handle these areas. The execution side is usually handled by a more junior staff member (Associate, Coordinator, or Specialist title) or outsourced at least in part to third parties, while the planning side is usually handled by someone more senior (Manager or Director level).

What They Do
All marketing campaigns begin with an objective. For example, the Vice President of Marketing might decide for strategic reasons that the company needs a lead generation campaign to win 20 new customers this year in an emerging market segment, and asks a Mar-

keting Programs Manager (MPM) to develop a plan – a *program* – to that end.

A common first step is that the MPM would build a mathematical model based on historical success rates, industry norms, and a healthy dose of assumptions and intuition to estimate how many leads he or she will need to generate in order to win 20 new deals. Such a model may predict, for instance, that for every 30 leads a particular type of marketing campaign generates, the company might close just one deal. That implies that the campaign will need to generate 600 leads (30 x 20) to win 20 customers.

Based on that target, the MPM will evaluate what specific marketing tactics will be most successful given the program's goals, budget, deadlines, and any factors that are unique to the customer segment being pursued. The MPM will frequently plan tactics in a certain sequence to maximize overall campaign effectiveness, as lead gen campaigns are usually more successful when prospective customers are reached multiple times through multiple channels (tactics). These decisions are rarely straightforward. For example, telemarketing is a very expensive and slow means of reaching out to prospects, and for most tech companies it's not particularly effective as a "first touch" in a campaign. However, telemarketing as a follow-up second or third touch in a series of integrated tactics can be highly effective. As another example, a well-executed email marketing campaign (analogous to direct mail, but done through email) can be executed very quickly and yield high response rates, but there are a multitude of issues regarding perceptions of spam, and the cost of acquiring valid, opted-in email addresses in the first place can be prohibitive. Such issues need to be carefully weighed in planning a campaign.

Once the appropriate marketing techniques are identified, the MPM must nail down the details. For instance, if direct mail will be used, what should the copy (the text of the letter) say? How many valid mailing addresses does the company already have and, if more are needed to reach the program target, how will those be acquired? How will leads generated through the mail portion of the campaign be tracked? What call to action will be presented in the mail piece? The list of questions such as these that need to be answered can be long.

Some of the work involved in executing the campaign may be outsourced to third parties if budgets permit or the company lacks in-house resources to accomplish the work. There are companies, for example, that specialize in writing compelling marketing copy, mail fulfillment (the actual printing and mailing of envelopes), telemarketing, print advertising design and placement, and many other services. Even if some of this work is outsourced, someone in the company needs to manage these vendors as well as perform some "internal" work, such as "scrubbing lists" (making sure that the postal mail or email addresses that will be contacted are up-to-date, complete, and relevant for this particular campaign).

A key part of an MPM's job is to track and report on data about the success of campaigns over time. Many of the metrics tracked relate to what is called a sales funnel. For instance, in a particular campaign, perhaps 10,000 emails were sent out; 9,000 were successfully received; 8,000 were opened; 6,000 people clicked-through to a webpage linked from the email; 2,000 people took the desired action on that webpage (such as registered to receive a free whitepaper); and of those 2,000 who received the paper, 100 entered into an active sales cycle with the company, of which 20 ultimately become customers. The MPM would need to evaluate the cost of this pro-gram against the revenue generated by those 20 new customers.

Useful Skills

Success at planning marketing programs requires broad familiarity with the full spectrum of marketing tactics available, coupled with a sense of intuition about what tactics will be most effective at meet-ing specific program goals. This kind of intuition can only be devel-oped through experience – both successes as well as failures. And MPMs need to have a certain personality. They must be willing to experiment and accept that some campaigns will simply not achieve the desired results. There are hundreds of documented best practices about this area, but it's important to understand that what works for one company or in one industry may not in another. Some companies find that email appeals to register for a free webi-nar get the best results for the money, while in another company direct mail campaigns to persuade people to attend a seminar are more effective.

MPMs must have strong interpersonal skills and be able to mo-tivate others to do what is needed for a campaign to come together successfully. In particular, it is critical that Marketing Programs Managers work well with the Sales team, especially Sales manage-ment. It's a symbiotic relationship. Many salespeople rely on lead gen programs to help them secure new business and meet their qu-otas, and Marketing usually relies on Sales to follow-up on leads to make them successful. Without Sales' buy-in and support, lead gen programs don't work.

MPMs must also work well with numerous other people or teams, both internally and externally. Product Marketers, for example, typically define the messaging behind product introduction campaigns, while Segment Marketers or Market Developers may define campaign messaging for particular markets. Externally, MPMs rarely work directly with customers but they frequently interact with third-party vendors to execute campaigns.

Quantitative skills and expertise using Microsoft Excel are also very important. As mentioned previously, MPMs need to build predictive models, and adjust existing models over time based on campaign successes and failures. Many tech companies drown in the amount of data they collect from their marketing programs, and a good MPM can sift through the data and hone in on the most important metrics for reporting purposes and to improve the effectiveness of future campaigns. Good MPMs also spot "red flags" in campaign performance, often before anyone else in the company realizes there may be a problem, and raise these issues with senior staff members before they become unfixable.

MPMs also tend to spend a lot of time "living in" whatever software tools their company uses for marketing automation, such as mass email marketing tools, customer relationship management (CRM) tools, sales force automation (SFA) tools, or various databases. (For a list of the most popular ones, see the Resources section on www.TechJobsBook.com.) If you don't already have experience using tools like these, you must be comfortable learning about such technologies.

Variations in Marketing Programs

There is incredible variety in the world of Marketing Programs regarding job titles and reporting structures.

You'll encounter titles such as Lead Generation Specialist, Demand Generation Manager, Demand Creation Manager, or Marketing Campaigns Manager. One software company calls it Field Marketing, even though it has nothing to do with Field Marketing as defined in Chapter 4. In some tech companies, Marketing Programs is just one of many functions managed by a MarCom Manager (see page 22).

In larger companies or those that rely heavily on marketing programs to generate leads, you may find more specialization. For example, some companies have Database Marketers whose full-time job is to continuously update and otherwise maintain the internal company databases that MPMs rely on. Or, at some companies, MPMs manage campaigns only for certain geographic territories, which are developed in conjunction with salespeople in that area (this is sometimes called "Regional MarCom" or similar). A relatively new position some tech companies are creating is called "Marketing Operations," which is similar to Sales Operations (chapter 17) but specifically focused on marketing programs.

Some companies (especially sales-driven companies) deem Marketing Programs to be so important that they have an entire team focused on it, with a dedicated Director who reports to the VP of Marketing. In other companies, the Marketing Programs function may be part of the MarCom group. Or, in small tech companies, MPMs may report directly to the VP of Marketing but "float," and not be formally part of any other group.

Career Paths

Most people in Marketing Programs begin their career more on the execution side than on the planning side. Many start with a generalist marketing background (often at the Associate or Specialist level) or have a Sales background (often Inside Sales). Some come from outside vendors such as direct mail fulfillment houses. As these individuals gain more experience and develop more intuition about what does and doesn't work, they typically move into a more strategic marketing programs planning role.

Marketing Programs is a good background for careers in Sales Operations, working for third-party vendors to which some aspects of programs are outsourced, or being an independent sales and marketing consultant. Because Marketing Programs touches so many areas within the Sales and Marketing organizations, it's also a great background for a Director or even VP-level Marketing position, especially in a sales-driven tech company.

CHAPTER TEN

Internet Marketing Management

Tech companies are increasingly embracing the Internet as a marketing channel that complement, or in some cases replaces, "traditional" outbound marketing channels such as direct mail, telemarketing and print media advertising. The primary function of an e-Marketing Manager (also commonly called an Internet Marketing Manager) is to manage all of the company's marketing activities that use the Web and email. This usually includes building and maintaining the company's public-facing website, as well as managing any marketing tools and campaigns that involve the Internet.

What an e-Marketer does – or whether one even exists in a company – depends largely on the size of the company. In small tech companies, there is often only one or two Marketing staff members, who will perform some of the tactical roles an e-Marketer normally performs as a small portion of their daily workload. As the company grows and marketing specialization becomes necessary, an e-Marketer may be hired who performs all of the roles described in the next section. But in very large companies, there may be multiple e-Marketers who perform some of those functions exclusively. Some large companies, for instance, have Email Marketing Managers who only handle the email side – not the Web side – of online marketing. Other companies have one or more individuals who focus solely on online advertising, and so on.

An e-Marketing Manager is not the same thing as a Webmaster. The one specific role people with either title may perform is the routine administrative maintenance and updating of a website. The key difference is that e-Marketing Managers are, foremost, marketing professionals and not information technology (IT) professionals. Webmasters, for instance, may directly access servers or databases that "power" the website for routine maintenance, while e-Marketers would generally don't touch the hardware and network side.

In fact, the larger the company is, the more the e-Marketer functions as a *marketer* and not as a Webmaster. Put differently, in smaller companies, the Marketing staff takes on many of the routine, tactical, Internet-related responsibilities that in a larger company a Webmaster would address.

Other similar job titles for this position include Interactive Marketing Manager, Online Marketing Manager, and Web Marketing Manager. They are all essentially identical.

What They Do

E-Marketing Managers perform a mix of administrative, consultative, and strategic roles. On the administrative or tactical side, the e-Marketer may, for example:

- Continually update the company's website when new press releases are issued or when new products are launched.
- Manage the company's content management system (CMS), which allows individuals throughout the company to upload or modify some website content on their own.

- Ensure that sales leads captured through Web and email marketing campaigns are correctly captured in the company's sales and marketing database.
- Compile, format and upload articles for incorporation into the company's email newsletters for current and prospective customers.
- Manage email marketing lists (add, delete, or change entries).
- Providing ongoing tracking and reporting of key website metrics (pageviews, click-throughs, etc.) to evaluate the success of sales and marketing initiatives.
- Test the appearance of your company's webpages and outbound emails in various Web browsers and email clients.

On the consultative side, e-Marketers provide strategic input to other Marketing team members regarding, for example, how best to:

- Track the success of an email marketing campaign.
- Modify the text on the website to improve the site's rankings with search engines (this is called Search Engine Optimization, or SEO).
- Write email newsletter content that will not be flagged by recipients' spam filters.

E-Marketers may also perform a host of more strategic roles that involve planning or implementing major new initiatives that involve the Internet, such as:

- Work with an outside media agency or Web design firm to create an entirely new corporate website.
- Implement a Search Engine Marketing (SEM) program to drive traffic to your website (also called pay-per-click, or PPC, advertising; this is what Google has made famous with the ads that appear alongside their search engine results).
- Plan and manage online advertising campaigns. (Tech companies that advertise heavily may have a separate role with a title like "Online Advertising Manager," or simply outsource all online ad placement activities to another firm.
- Help the company implement a strategy to capitalize on "Web 2.0" technologies such as podcasts, blogs, RSS feeds, user-submitted content, and social networking sites.
- Identify and implement new techniques to use the Internet's global reach to build awareness about the company.
- Implement tactics to "convert" casual website visitors into sales leads.
- Write business cases to justify investments in new online initiatives or software technologies.

Useful Skills

Internet Marketing Management is a semi-technical role with several requisite skill areas.

On the technical side, you should know how to write and edit HTML (the scripting language of the Web) using rich text editors. You should also be familiar with how cascading style sheets (CSS) work. In addition, you should be well-versed in the field of usability – how to design webpages so that they're easy to use.

E-Marketers need to have an eye for design. Although you may not be designing websites, you need to know good design from bad when you see it. Some background in design or other area of art is thus extremely useful. This will help you ensure, among other things, that webpages are well laid out and use appropriate colors, and that email newsletters grab recipients' attention quickly with an enticing design. You should also be familiar with popular website design tools.

In addition, you need to be broadly familiar with third-party software systems that store or use customer data captured through Web- and email-based marketing campaigns. This includes customer relationship management (CRM) systems; sales and marketing automation systems; mass email marketing tools; and content management systems. (For a continuously updated list of the more popular ones, visit the Resources section of www.TechJobsBook.com). These Web-based or offline software packages are often tightly integrated into tech companies' online marketing efforts. The data captured through your company's website often will be transferred, whether through automated or manual means, into one of these systems.

Finally, you should understand how to interpret Internet marketing metrics, as well as the limitations of Web statistical tracking software. Mining the vast amounts of data captured online automatically is a key role for e-Marketers.

Career Paths

Most e-Marketers have a mixed background encompassing some kind of design (Web design, graphic design, or a similar field) and

hands-on experience with Internet technologies (website development, content management systems, email systems, etc.). But e-
Marketers are, foremost, marketing professionals. As such, they also need some experience with general marketing concepts, whether
obtained through coursework or by experience.

E-Marketer positions generally require a Bachelor's degree (in
any field) and a few years of work experience, though specific academic or professional credentials are less important than being able
to show a portfolio of related work, and particularly before-and-
after results – for instance, showing a website you redesigned and
documenting the increase in website traffic after it went live.

To become an e-Marketing Manager, you should obtain training
or work experience in whatever areas mentioned above that you're
weak. If you're fairly Internet savvy, it's relatively easy to learn
about specific new technologies and tools just by reading books or
taking short courses. In particular, you should learn about the more
popular sales force automation tools and any content management
system (there are many, and they all work similarly). Gaining
knowledge about good design and usability practices or marketing
techniques is best accomplished through work experience, but
again there are good books and courses that can help hone these
skills.

It's important to note that e-Marketers must continually stay on
top of new technologies, since technology changes so quickly.
Whether you're trying to get into the field or once you're already in
it, you will need to track what's happening in the online tools world
by visiting certain websites, reading trade journals or attending
conferences.

E-marketing is a good springboard for other careers in tech marketing, especially in companies that rely heavily on the Web and email for new customer acquisition, such as "dotcom" websites – in which almost everyone in the Marketing team is, to some extent, involved in e-marketing. E-marketing is also a good background for managing marketing programs, since so many marketing campaigns at tech companies are intertwined between traditional marketing channels and online channels.

CHAPTER ELEVEN

Corporate Communications

All members of the Marketing and Sales teams of a tech company communicate to varying degrees with the outside world,
whether by speaking directly with customers, participating in public events like trade shows, writing articles for trade journals, or re-
leasing marketing materials on the company's website. However,
all such communications are targeted at current or prospective customers. Someone needs to manage outbound communications in-
tended for everyone else – the general public, the media, industry
analysts, and many other groups. This is the role of Corporate
Communications ("CorpComm") Managers.

Some tech companies use the terms "CorpComm Manager" and
"Public Relations (PR) Manager" interchangeably, while some
companies draw a distinction between these roles. In general, PR
Managers communicate only with external audiences (primarily the
media), while CorpComm Managers may *in addition* deal with internal audiences (employees). Some companies have people with
the title of Internal Communications Manager to signify that they
do not work with external audiences at all.

Another related job title is Investor Relations (IR) Manager. This
position only exists at companies that are publicly traded on the
stock market, or will soon file to go public. IR Managers serve as
the single point of contact for inquiries from current or prospective
investors (ranging from an individual investor to a large financial

institution), and IR Managers create all communications that go out to investors, such as prospectus.

Individuals in all three roles may be referred to as "Communications Managers." They all generally have strong communication skills in writing, editing and speaking, and as such may be called upon by other groups within the company to assist with a range of projects beyond the typical scope of their duties.

CorpComm is usually the high-level blanket description of all of these similar but distinct titles. A very large tech company may have a CorpComm department, with sub-departments or individuals specifically focused on external (PR), internal, and investor (IR) audiences. Small tech companies typically have a single Corp-Comm Manager, while very large companies may have a separate Manager for every product line, or every geographic region the company does business in.

Note that CorpComm may not be a part of the Marketing organization. Some companies, sometimes smaller ones but usually only larger ones, separate this function and have a VP of Corp-Comm. In most small- to mid-sized tech companies, however, a Director of CorpComm or Senior CorpComm Managers report to the VP of Marketing.

What They Do
CorpComm Managers facilitate communication on what the company is doing to *external* audiences – generally, everyone *other than* current or prospective customers. These Managers work with the media, industry analysts, and a range of "influencers" who can sway public opinions, such as bloggers and consultants. Some

CorpComm Managers appropriately describe their job as "reputation management."

CorpComm Managers also work internally with executives and other senior managers who might speak to the outside world to ensure they stay "on message." To this end, CorpComm Managers often prepare briefing documents of various kinds which serve as "cheat sheets" for employees to use when speaking to the outside world.

One of the more common activities that CorpComm Managers in tech companies are known for is writing press releases. Indeed, in some small tech companies this is all they do. These press releases typically report on new product announcements, major customer wins, recent executive hires, awards the company has recently received, or any upcoming event in which the company will participate – anything to help position the company favorably in the public's mind.

Savvy tech companies realize that "reporting" news is only half the game. One of the arts of CorpComm is helping to shape media coverage to reflect positively on the company. For instance, rather than hoping that a particular industry trade publication simply reprints excerpts from your press release, as a CorpComm Manager you could call a reporter at that media outlet, convince him or her to write an in-depth story about your company, and subtly persuade him or her to include details or quotes that make your company shine in the best light. "Pitching stories" in this way is a major role of most CorpComm Managers. Most reporters typically receive literally hundreds of news releases or email "pitches" a day. It is the job of the CorpComm Manager to help make his or her company's news stand out from the rest.

In addition to media stories, most CorpComm Managers pitch speaking opportunities for company executives or other senior staff members, as well. Getting your company's employees "face time" with large audiences is an effective way to keep your company top of mind with different audiences. These speaking opportunities may be at industry conferences, networking events, or even informal luncheons. Pitching a speaking opportunity usually involves writing a compelling statement of who will speak (a speaker bio) and the topic, as well as what the audience will learn or gain from hearing this presentation. Particularly at larger tech companies, some CorpComm Managers also write speeches for executives, create their presentations in Microsoft PowerPoint, and even coach them on presentation skills.

Another area in which CorpComm Managers frequently get involved is submitting award nominations. Every industry has well-regarded awards. For example, there are several awards given by a variety of organizations to companies or non-profits with great websites. Software companies that make technical components for those websites will frequently nominate their customers' websites for such awards, and then share in some of the recognition if that website wins, with a claim that "we helped build that award-winning website." There are also awards that are company-specific, rather than product-specific. For instance, there are a variety of "fastest growing company" awards in certain industries or geographic areas, which recognize corporate achievements.

Press releases, shaping media opinions, and pitching speaking opportunities and awards represent the bulk of what CorpComm Managers do on a day-to-day basis. But the work these managers perform can be sporadic – most of the time routine, but punctuated by waves of prolonged, intense activity before and during the occurrence of key events or changes. For instance, these managers are one of the first to know internally when a company plans on making an acquisition, merging with another company, launching or discontinuing a major new product line, entering or retreating from a market, or laying off employees. During these times of transitions, Communications Managers are called upon to craft tightly-controlled, public- or inward-facing communications to release the news in whatever way the company feels is best.

For example, during an acquisition, employees at both companies will have concerns about layoffs; customers of the acquired company will have concerns about interruptions in their service; the media will want to know what the story is; and investors will have concerns regarding just about everything. In such a situation, CorpComm Managers will spend weeks or months preparing communication plans for those various audiences, defining precisely what will be conveyed to whom, how, and when. Employees may be given a confidential FAQ (Frequently Asked Questions) document that addresses the most likely concerns employees will have; customers will receive personal phone calls from the CEO to assure them not to worry; key contacts in the media may be given an exclusive on the story and briefed ahead of time, while everyone else in the media will just receive a press release; and investors may need to be sent legal documents seeking their approval of an acquisition.

Useful Skills

Let's start with the obvious: communication professionals need to be good communicators. In particular, they need to be able to write and edit effectively, though at larger companies these individuals may be called upon to speak in public, too.

Being able to communicate things well is critical, but so is being able to determine *what* to communicate and *when*, as well as having good intuition when it is better to say nothing at all. Communications managers are first and foremost marketing professionals. Like any marketing manager, they need to be good at the art of positioning their company in the best possible light. That requires an ability to "get inside the heads" of all the constituencies to whom they will communicate. It also requires a healthy dose of strategic planning skill and acute attention to detail. CorpComm is not for those who don't obsess about finding just the right word to express an important point.

Another skill set that it is increasingly sought by employers is familiarity with digital media – specifically, blogs, podcasting, and social networking sites. Understanding the technology behind these tools isn't critical. You need to know what's out there and, more importantly, how to use these tools, websites and the people behind them to help strengthen your company's reputation.

To work at a tech company in a CorpComm area does not require technical proficiency with the company's products, but a general level of technical competence is quite helpful. When a PR Manager is writing a press release to announce a new product launch, he or she will typically work with a Product Manager or Product Marketer to decide what features and product capabilities should be highlighted. Those conversations will go more smoothly if the

CorpComm Manager has at least a modicum level of understanding of the technologies in question, why the new product's feature set is important, how customers will benefit, and how the new product is differentiated from what competitors offer. Don't be too concerned if you don't already have these skills; learning about the company's technologies will happen naturally with time. More important is that you have a willingness to learn.

Career Paths

Most CorpComm professionals have degrees in journalism, public relations, communications, marketing or a related field. Tech companies often hire undergraduates in these fields as interns to work under a CorpComm employee, and they may be offered a full-time position upon graduation.

Another common entry point is through a PR agency, particularly one that works with tech clients. Many agencies give their employees exposure to a wide range of clients, and the breadth of that background is appealing to many companies. Other CorpComm professionals have prior experience in broadcast journalism, speechwriting, freelance writing or editing, or other communications-related areas.

Common "next step" career paths for Corporate Communications professionals include managing CorpComm for a larger company (the CorpComm needs of a multi-billion dollar, publicly traded multinational are very different from a small, privately held software company), working in a senior-level position for a PR agency, becoming an independent communications consultant, or specializing in a particular communications area such as speech-writing.

CHAPTER TWELVE

Events Management

Almost all tech companies, once they reach a certain size, participate in events. In this context, events include but are not limited to industry trade shows, conferences, seminars, webinars (seminars conducted online and viewed by participants through a web browser and telephone). Involvement in an event such as these is done for a business purpose (usually to acquire prospective customer leads or to generate awareness in the market about the company) but they can also be for internal purposes, such as company staff meetings, customer conferences, or recruiting events. Event staff plan and manage the company's participation in such events.

A company's involvement in an event may be limited or broad. For example, it might send a single individual to a trade show just to scope out the competition. Or, it might choose to exhibit at a trade show and send a small team to staff the booth. Or, it might exhibit at the show, co-exhibit at partners' booths, co-sponsor the show financially, arrange offsite luncheons for VIP attendees, build a special product to demo at the show, and much more.

Most tech companies either hold or attend one or two big events each year. For example, most mid-sized or larger software companies hold an annual user's conference. The Events Manager's job becomes far more complex when the company participates in events throughout the year. Each event can take months of planning, and the event planning process for one event will often overlap with the next few events.

The process becomes even more complex when partners or other third parties are involved. For example, a company may be hosting a conference that will include five panels of five speakers each, representing a variety of customers, partners and industry analysts. The Events Manager will thus need to coordinate schedules and all communications among up to 25 people, from several different organizations. As inevitably happens, at least one person will end up needing to cancel his or her participation due to a work or personal conflict. Someone will miss their flight to the conference. Someone will lose their laptop with all their PowerPoint slides on it. And so on. Event Managers need to plan for all such contingencies.

As with most Marketing disciplines, there is both a strategic and a tactical side to Events. The strategic components – determining which events to participate in, establishing budgets, assigning resources, and so on – is generally managed by more senior Marketing staff, such as a Senior Events Manager or a Director of Marketing Communications (to whom Events staff members usually report in a mid-sized or larger company). The more tactical elements of "executing" an event are usually handled by more junior staff members at the Coordinator or Specialist job title level. In smaller companies, there may only be one Events person who handles both, or a single MarCom Manager may handle events as just one part of a wider range of duties.

What They Do

It's important to keep the strategic and tactical elements of event management separate. The strategic piece involves developing an Event plan that supports both sales objectives and broader company goals, under the constraints of limited staff and financial resources. Events Managers need to understand those goals and constraints and create a plan and event calendar, sometimes up to a year or more in advance of the events. The plan outlines what events the company will participate in, what the goals for company participation in each event are, and what resources (people, equipment, money, etc.) are required.

The Events Manager will typically work with all other members of the Marketing team to ensure that the events they're planning to be involved in complement other marketing plans. For example, if a Market Developer is planning a major push into a new market segment six months from now, the Events Manager may plan an event to coincide with that push. Or, a Marketing Programs Manager may work closely with the Events Manager to filter invitation lists and get the word about an event through direct mail, email, or telephone calls. And, if partners are in any way involved in the event, the Partner Marketer will work closely with the Events Manager, too.

Salespeople tend to want the company to participate in every event in which they can get face time with prospective customers. A key role of an Events Manager is to negotiate with Sales, sometimes on an individual salesperson basis, on what events the company should participate in from a lead generation standpoint. There are always trade-offs – this show will attract a lot of prospects but is extremely expensive to exhibit at, while this conference will have a lower quantity but higher quality turnout and the company can sponsor it for a very low cost, and we only have budget to do one of these two events.

Once event plans are finalized, more strategically focused Event Managers rely on others internally (usually Event Coordinators) to manage the exhaustive list of tactical steps necessary to participate in events. A sampling of these tactical responsibilities includes:

- Registering the company and personnel for events.
- Securing hotel rooms, conference rooms, booths and booth equipment, and ground transportation for people and materials.
- Shipping materials, such as marketing collateral or equipment, to the event location.
- Briefing company attendees on event logistics, key messaging, or other important issues before they leave.
- Working with third-party vendors to create special materials or products for a particular event, such as giveaway products (sometimes called "swag") or special collateral.
- Working with other Marketing team members to invite the company's prospects to attend events, whether by mail, email, or phone call.
- Keeping the company's senior management apprised of who attended the event, what the response was, etc.
- Tracking all event-related expenses against budget.
- Assisting invited attendees with registrations, travel arrangements, cancellations, etc.

- Pitching speak opportunities for key personnel to speak at events hosted by other parties. (Corporate Communications Managers may also do this.)
- Verifying key attendee availability. Personnel who need to attend a certain event can't be traveling on business or on vacation when they're needed.

Event Coordinators may also work with outside materials suppliers or event planning companies. There are hundreds of companies that make everything from trade show booths to giveaway products (like pens with your company name on them), as well as companies that create personalized invitations and print collateral, generate buzz in the media about your event, cater food and drinks to events, and much more.

Useful Skills

At the strategic level, Event Managers need to have a broad understanding of the sales and marketing functions, as well as business in general. They must be able to align event plans with corporate goals, make trade-off analyses, and be comfortable making tough decisions about allocating limited resources.

Good interpersonal skills are also important, at both the strategic and tactical levels. You must be polite, friendly, flexible and highly personable to get people to take action and help you when needed. At the same time, you need to be able to become firm and slightly aggressive so that you can push others when they're not meeting their deadlines or other obligations, such as giving you their biography for submission to a speaking opportunity. Diplomacy and negotiation skills go a long way in this role, too.

At the tactical level, a high level of attention to detail and superior organizational skills are of paramount importance. This is especially true when a company participates in multiple events concurrently or throughout the year.

Event management also requires some software competencies. Microsoft Project is frequently used to coordinate complex events; Microsoft Excel is often used to track event-related expenses; and online event registration tools and webinar tools are also commonly used. As mentioned in other Marketing chapters, more and more Marketing organizations rely on customer relationship management (CRM) tools to manage their customer databases, which in turn dictates who is invited to certain events and whether they attended. It's thus helpful to be familiar with all such tools, or have a willingness and capability to learn new systems.

Career Paths

Event Managers typically rise to the strategic level after two-to-five years of successful experience on the tactical side of events. Most people start off in Events as an Intern, managing the most tactical aspects of events, such as processing registrations and mailing out invitations. Interns who perform well are often extended offers to join the company full-time upon graduation at a Specialist or Coordinator level.

Some Events staff are hired from companies that focus exclusively on planning and running events for other companies on a contract basis. Many individuals start off at these "events only" companies as Interns or Associates. This kind of background can be invaluable to tech companies, as these individuals already have broad experience with several companies.

Admittedly, career advancement in the Events area is somewhat limited. Many Events Managers get "pigeon-holed." They can certainly manage more and more events, or manage larger events, or become involved in international event planning, or build and manage a large Events team. But, in the end, it's all still about events. So, after a "tour of duty" in Events, many people move on to other areas in the MarCom side of the house, especially in Marketing Programs or Partner Marketing because events are often an integral part of those areas.

CHAPTER THIRTEEN

The Sales Organization

Y ou probably have an accurate notion of what Sales is all about because you have undoubtedly worked with salespeople before. Salespeople are the face of the company to prospective customers. Whether selling software, hardware, cars or shoes, salespeople do basically the same thing: persuade people to buy your company's products and services.

Not all tech companies have sales forces, or even a single salesperson. In very small companies, a key executive (often the CEO) may handle all selling. This is possible because most small companies can only take on a handful of customers at one time, and one individual can handle a sales pipeline of just a few customers. As the company grows, however, the pipeline becomes too large for one individual to cover on his or her own.

It isn't just a function of the number of customers. Many vendors of Web-based services with countless thousands of customers don't have salespeople, either. To place ads on Google, for example, you can simply visit their website, learn about your options, sign-up online and pay using a credit card. No people are involved in this entire process.

Generally speaking, tech companies have salespeople when any of the following apply:

- **The product or service being delivered is non-standardized**. Dell can sell computer equipment over the Internet because the individual parts that make its computers are all standardized. A buyer can easily compare the technical specifications, pricing, warranties, and case designs of a Dell PC versus a Hewlett-Packard PC on his or her own; talking to a salesperson would add little value. But if the product were unique from all competitors, did things that were unfamiliar to most buyers (everyone knows what a PC does), could be heavily customized, and had a negotiable (not fixed) price, a salesperson could be useful and, in fact, might be necessary.

- **The customers' needs are complex and require some analysis and consultation**. Some tech companies make software that is so highly customizable that no two customers have an identical installation of it, or use it in the same way. Customers buying complex technology – or customers with complex needs – often require some "hand holding" by salespeople to help them pinpoint exactly what they should buy to meet their goals and how it should be customized for their specific needs.

- **The market is new and requires people to "evangelize" the benefits of the company's products or services**. Even if the product *could* be sold over the phone or through a website, some products require a live demonstration or personal consultation to convey its purpose and value.

- **The cost of the product or service is significant, and no customer would pay that much without some personal attention**. Dell will sell a computer to an individual like you through its website, without you having to talk to a salesperson. But if Dell is trying to sell 10,000 computers to a government agency, a salesperson (or a team of them) will surely be involved.

Structure of the Sales Organization

Sales organizations in tech companies are broadly organized into three groups: people who sell (salespeople), people who support the salespeople (sales operations and sales engineering), and people who manage these two groups (sales management).

Salespeople can be broadly grouped into one of two categories: entry-level or experienced. The *usual* job title given to entry-level salespeople is Associate, and the *usual* job title given to more experienced salespeople is Executive – but see "Job Titles" below for more information on this.

Sales departments usually also include individuals who are not salespeople. At a minimum, most software and some hardware companies have Sales Engineers (Chapter 16), and most medium-sized or larger tech companies have Sales Operations Managers (Chapter 17). Some Sales departments have other roles, which are not detailed in this book. For instance, some Sales teams have people with titles such as Project Manager who assist the team with implementing a variety of short-term projects. Some teams also have people who continuously train and coach the team on effective selling strategies.

The roles of Sales Managers are straightforward. Sales organizations are usually hierarchical. Salespeople tend to be grouped either by:

- Territory (geographic region)
- Market/vertical they sell to (for example, Education clients)
- Size of account they sell to (Small Business versus Enterprise)
- Function (Inside Sales versus Outside Sales)

All the salespeople in one of these groups usually reports to a Sales Director. For instance, all the salespeople located in the Midwestern states may report to a Regional Sales Director for the Midwest. All the Directors report to the VP of Sales.

Sales Management, as a role, is not detailed in this book. Suffice it to say, however, that Sales Managers (or Directors, or VPs) reach their positions by being good at selling. They "move up the ranks" by consistently meeting or exceeding their quotas, and by helping their fellow salespeople do so, too.

Job Titles in Sales

A customer's perception of whom they're buying from is important. Customers like to feel that the salesperson assigned to them is a senior, seasoned sales professional. It conveys a sentiment that the company cares enough about winning their business to assign one of their best people to work with them. To that end, salespeople are often given somewhat glorified titles such as Senior Account Executive to convey that sentiment when, in fact, every customer gets the same level of salesperson. This can be especially confusing because although the term "executive" anywhere else in a company refers to a member of the executive management team, in a Sales organization it can refer to any salesperson.

Adding to the confusion is that some tech companies give their salespeople titles that mean something completely different at another company. At one software company in Austin, *every* Sales Executive holds the title Director of Business Development. None of them does traditional business development as defined in Chapter 7, and none are Directors as the title is typically used in tech companies (they have no direct reports). A different software company uses the title Market Development Associate to mean Sales Associate – they don't do "market development" at all as defined in Chapter 5.

The titles given to those in sales support and sales management generally *do* follow the same career ladder structure as in Marketing – Manager, Director, and VP.

The Two Main Categories of Salesperson

Regardless of their exact title, salespeople in tech companies are generally only segmented into two levels. You will see different names for these levels, but most companies refer to more junior salespeople as "Inside Sales" or "Associates," while more experienced salespeople are usually called "Field Sales" or "Executives."

Whatever the title, all salespeople do basically the same thing: serve as a customer's primary point of contact at a tech company throughout the sales process. The term "primary" is important because the customer may also interact with other people in your organization in that sales process, such as with Sales Engineers, Associate Account Executives, Marketing staff members, Professional Services staff, or corporate executives. It's thus helpful to think of the Sales Executive as a sort of "team leader" who coordinates the sales process internally to ensure that the company puts its best foot forward for the prospective customer.

While Marketing titles and career paths tend to correlate with one's years of experience, nature or quality of experience, education, and subjective assessments of individuals, one's rank in a Sales organization hinges almost entirely on one issue: how well you can sell. To generalize things, Associates are usually hired into a Sales organization at a tech company either with no sales experience whatsoever, two years or less selling a related product, or a few more years of sales experience but not in tech. Executives are usually hired with *at least* two years of demonstrably successful, relevant selling experience.

There are widespread exceptions to these generalities. I have seen a Harvard MBA with ten years of work experience (though none of it in Sales) become a Sales Executive. And I have seen a Human Resources Director with ten years of work experience switch careers and start over as a Sales Associate.

Virtually everyone who begins a sales career – regardless of other work experience – is initially placed on a form of probation. They need to prove they can sell effectively and meet a sales quota. If they do well in their first two or three quarters, they can stay. If they do well for several consecutive sales quarters, they move up. If they fail at any point, they're often fired or asked to transfer elsewhere in the company. Sales can be painfully cut-throat.

Compensation

Salespeople have a more complex compensation structure than those in Marketing. There are usually three components:

- **Base pay (salary)** is a set amount that a company regularly pays to an employee regardless of his or her individual performance or that of the entire Sales team. Base pay levels vary tremendously, though in most Sales organizations the base pay is on the low end of the scale for those of similar experience levels. If it weren't, salespeople would have less incentive to work harder to earn a commission.

- **Commissions** are a percentage of the total value of a sale that is paid to the employee by the company. For instance, if a salesperson has a 10% commission rate, he or she would earn $100 for every $1,000 dollars worth of goods or services sold to a customer. Commission rates vary widely, as does the timing of the payouts; commissions may be paid in one lump sum at the end of a quarter, or only when a customer pays its invoices, or some other timing schedule may be used.

- **Bonuses and incentives** are a general class of compensation which is used to motivate salespeople to reach certain sales goals, usually with a competitive aspect built in. For example, a Sales Manager may give an on-the-spot $1,000 cash bonus to the first salesperson to sell a certain quantity of hardware. Or, anyone who exceeds their quota by 50% may get a company car or a trip to the Caribbean.

Commissions and bonuses may be split among multiple people. For example, an Associate who does some initial selling to a prospect in a deal that is later closed by an Executive may get a portion of the commission due the Executive. The split may be a fixed percentage (say, 50%/50%) or a sliding scale based on the relative contribution each member of this team made to closing the deal. These kinds of sharing deals may be a matter of company policy or may be negotiated on the side between two or more members of the Sales team.

It's also worth noting that Sales Managers all the way up to the VP of Sales typically get compensated, in part, based on the performance of their team members below them. It surprises some to know that the VP of Sales at many tech companies makes more than the CEO.

CHAPTER FOURTEEN

Sales Executive / Field Sales

Sales Executives are sometimes called "Field Sales" in situations where they are geographically based in an office remote from the company's headquarters, or if they are based at the headquarters but travel extensively to call on customers. Put differently, they work "out in the field," as opposed to most Associate-level salespeople, who are typically based at the company's headquarters and do most of their selling over the phone.

What They Do

It's hard to generalize what Sales Executives do, because it varies tremendously based on the industry, types of customers, complexity of the product, and many other factors. But, at the highest level, a Sales Executive learns about a customer's needs and proposes a package of products (and usually services) to meet those needs. The "package" is generally presented in the form of a proposal, and in a tech company, the proposal usually includes more than simply a list of products or services that meet the customer's needs and a price quote – it also often includes details of how the products will be implemented for that particular customer, deployment timelines, payment terms, details of post-sale customer support, and much more. These proposals can be extremely long and detailed, especially for a complex or very expensive sale.

The tactical steps leading up to the submission of a proposal can be anything from quick and simple to long and multi-faceted. Once a sales cycle has begun, a sampling of things Sales Executives may "do" includes:

- Meet with multiple employees of the prospective customer to introduce the company and its products, as well as to build consensus that his or her company is the one they should buy from.
- Present materials created by the Marketing organization to showcase the value of the company's products. These may include documents such as PowerPoint presentations, return-on-investment calculations, customer testimonials and case studies, and customized whitepapers.
- Help prospective customers identify and prioritize their biggest problems, and then position the company to be the best vendor to alleviate those problems.
- "Wine and dine" prospective customers (which these days usually just means have lunch with them) to build rapport.
- Frequently but subtly point out shortcomings in competitors' products to bias prospective customers in favor of his or her company.
- Solicit questions and concerns from prospective customers, then either address them or route them to others in the company and report back to the prospect.

Few salespeople only work one sales cycle at a time. And, while pursuing multiple deals, salespeople must also continuously be looking for their next deal to pursue. To that end, Sales Executives might, for instance, work closely with Marketing to define new lead generation campaigns, build relationships with channel partners (if the company sources leads through third parties), cold call on prospects, research potential target customers, and attend trade shows or conferences to seek out prospects.

Useful Skills

What it takes to be good at sales in a tech company isn't that different from what it takes to be good at sales in any other industry. Unfortunately, there are hundreds of books on what it takes to be good at sales, and there's little agreement on what the top few skills are. Sure, you need to be good at listening to prospective customers' needs and wants, you need to be persuasive, you need to have some "guts" and be aggressive when appropriate. Beyond these more obvious attributes, most tech companies do look for a few specific things, however.

First, familiarity with certain formal sales methodologies is often sought. The most popular one in tech is called "Solution Selling," but every tech company has its favorite, usually based on the preferences of the VP of Sales. New books come out every few months that espouse a new selling methodology or a variant of an existing one, and some Sales Managers will direct their teams to follow it. Sales Executives who are already familiar with the methodology *du jour* might have an edge in getting hired.

Another specific skill sought by most tech companies is comfort selling to all levels of an organization. Sales Executives selling technology products often need to influence individuals at the target company. These individuals range from C-level executives who must approve the purchase (if expensive) down to those who will be the ultimate end-users of the products (who may not have a final say in the purchase decision but must still "buy in" to it).

Experience selling the particular products or services the company sells never hurts but is usually not an absolute requirement. However, experience selling *some* kind of technology product is usually desired, if for no other reason that it suggests the salesperson can "talk shop" with others in the company about technology-related products.

Career Paths

As discussed in the introductory chapter on Sales, there is no "common" or "best" background for a Sales career. The best way to get into Sales is to jump in anywhere and get your feet wet. Regardless of your prior experience – if you have any at all – the best starting point is to become an Associate Sales Executive (see next chapter) at a technology company. Ideally, start at a company that will team you up with a Sales Executive, or one that offers a formal sales training program to develop your skills.

If you're successful at selling, you'll eventually move up into a Sales Executive role or into sales management. Sales positions, at any level, are also excellent preparation for a career in Marketing. Good marketers understand the sales process and the needs of the Sales team, and those who worked in Sales are in the best position to know that.

Sales also is outstanding preparation for a position as CEO. In tech, few things are regarded as highly as the ability to sell effectively.

CHAPTER FIFTEEN

Associate Sales Executive / Inside Sales

The entry-level sales position in most tech companies is called an Associate, an Inside Sales Executive, or Inside Sales Associate. The term "inside" refers to the fact that most Associate (Inside) sales representatives are based at the company's headquarters and don't leave the office to sell. They're literally inside the building as opposed to out in the field. They do the majority of their selling work over the phone, whether through inbound calls (by customers calling in over the toll-free number) or outbound calling (cold calling). Thus, yet another title for this role is "Telesales."

You'll encounter all kinds of other titles for this type of salesperson – Sales Associate, Associate Business Developer, and Associate Market Developer. Regardless of the exact phrasing, if the words "Associate" or "Inside" are in the job title, most of what's in this chapter will describe the role. For simplicity, I'll use the word "Associate" throughout this chapter.

Compared to Sales Executives, Associates tend to focus on selling lower-priced products, in deals worth less in total value, or to smaller customers (individuals, or small and medium sized-businesses, also called SMBs).

Even though it's an entry-level position for those with zero-to-three years of sales experience, at many tech companies an Associate sales role offers a great foray into the world of sales. Associates are sometimes paired up with a more senior salesperson,

110 Sales and Marketing Careers

from whom they can "learn the ropes." Associates are also generally given a healthy amount of training, both in terms of sales skills and in the technologies their company sells.

Contrasting Associates and Executives

Sales Associates essentially do what Sales Executives do, with the notable difference that Associates aren't out selling in the field.

The basic sales processes are the same, too, but Associates typically juggle more customers simultaneously and close deals faster because the price levels are lower and the customer organizations are smaller, thus can make purchase decisions faster.

Another difference is that many Associates work during normal business hours at the company's offices, while Executives inevitably work irregular hours due to travel schedules.

A final difference is that Associates often can get ample assistance, and quickly, from others in the company because they're typically based in an office in close proximity to other Inside Salespeople, Sales Managers, and the Marketing team. In contrast, Executives typically work from home or from a small remote office, and getting assistance from headquarters might require waiting for a return phone call.

A Hybrid Team Sales Model

In most tech companies, the Inside and Outside sales teams operate autonomously in parallel, with Inside salespeople focusing on smaller deals and Outside teams focusing on larger deals. A variant of this is for an Associate to be paired up with an Executive to form a joint selling team. In this model, the Associate and Executive divide up the sales tasks at various points in the sales cycle, and ultimately split the sales commission if the deal is won. I suspect this model will become increasingly popular, so it's worth describing here.

Not surprisingly, the parts of the sales cycle the less experienced Associate gets to handle are usually the ones that the more senior Executive doesn't want to do. But let's keep this in perspective. Salespeople at tech companies are *very* expensive to employ, when their salaries, commissions, and travel expenses are factored in. And the better the salesperson is at closing business, the more expensive he or she is to employ. As such, companies want their best salespeople to focus on the hardest parts of the sales process, which usually come toward the end – meeting with the most senior executives at the prospect company, convincing the prospect to commit to the purchase as soon as possible, and commanding the highest price possible. In this hybrid model, Executives rely on Associates to do most of the legwork that gets the Executive into those high-level meetings and contract negotiations.

Associates typically are most active in the first two stages of the sales process, prospecting and qualification. Prospecting is all about finding new customers. In the prospecting stage, the Associate may cold call key target accounts, work with the Marketing department (usually Marketing Programs Managers) to develop targeted prospecting campaigns via e-mail, direct mail, or telemarketing, and network at professional events. Sales Executives are usually involved in these activities, too, but to a lesser extent. For example, the Executive and Associate may jointly define or prioritize prospect target lists before the Associate starts calling on them.

Qualification entails delving into the customer's needs, budget, and timeline to understand how good a fit this customer is for the company. In the qualification stage, the Associate has to make some tricky decisions about to what extent a prospect is truly interested in buying the company's products, and when, and how much the prospect can really afford. Most Associates will immediately pass on leads to their Executive when the prospect would be a huge strategic win, is desperate for a solution, and has a huge budget already allotted. Of course, such a "nirvana" situation is rare. Even when a prospect says they're "ready to move quickly" or "the budget for this is already authorized," it's usually either not true or only partially true. At the same time, Associates face the risk of ignoring such leads when the prospect is actually reflecting their situation accurately. An Associate will thus usually work carefully with his or her Executive to discern the best opportunities to pursue while "back burnering" the rest.

Some Associates do manage entire deal cycles on their own. Whether and when this happens is usually negotiated between the Executive and Associate. The Associate will often need to first earn the Executive's trust before the Executive turns over the reins. After this evaluation period, an Executive may allow the Associate, for example, to pursue any deals under a certain price point, simpler deals involving a limited product range, or deals with smaller customers.

Associates also play a critical role in coordinating communications with prospects. The sales process in tech companies tends to be extremely document-heavy. Many prospects will request formal proposals, technical specifications, brochures, copies of PowerPoint presentations, whitepapers, contracts and much more. Many of these things are created by Marketing and can simply be e-mailed to a prospect, but I have yet to see a tech sales cycle in which the prospect didn't request some customized materials or information. The Associate might or might not be the person who creates these materials, but he or she is usually the person who identifies the internal staff resource to create them, and is then subsequently responsible for communicating it back to the prospect.

A final general role the Associate performs is interfacing with other internal groups during the sales cycle. For example, an Associate may work with Sales Engineers to schedule a demo for the prospect, or coordinate with a company executive to schedule a meeting or phone call with the CEO at the prospect company. Associates are in a good position to do this, since Associates are usually based at the company's headquarters while many Executives are geographically distributed or frequently traveling.

Useful Skills
The skills that make a good Associate are not significantly different than those that make a good Executive, but there are a few notable differences. First, an Executive has to be very comfortable in personal interactions, while it's less common for Associates to meet with prospects.

Second, Associates need to be comfortable making cold calls. Even some of the most seasoned Executive aren't good at this.

Third, Associates have to be extremely discriminating during the prospecting and qualifying stages. In a sense, Executives have an easier time in that if they were able to get a foot-in-the-door meeting with a key decision maker, the prospect is probably legitimately interested. In contrast, Associates spend a lot of time having initial conversations with prospects over the phone, many of which lead nowhere.

Other, more generally useful skills for an Associate include being able to write well (because they craft so many emails, proposals, and other documents) and being extremely organized (because most Associates juggle multiple prospects concurrently). They should also be technically adept at using software tools such as sales automation software and proposal generation tools.

Career Paths

There is no common career path into Sales. At the Associate level, most tech companies require a Bachelor's degree (in any field), or at least two years of successful work experience. *Any* kind of customer-facing sales experience is useful and highly desirable, be it retail sales, door-to-door sales, telemarketing, and so forth. It matters much less what you sold, more that you sold it well. Of course, experience selling technology products is preferable to having sold, say, refrigerators, but most tech companies would still rather hire the guy who sold millions of dollars worth of fridges than the guy who sold thousands of dollars of software.

If you're considering a career in Sales, keep in mind that your performance will be evaluated almost entirely by how much you sell. Period. It won't matter that you're a nice person, had a good attitude, tried really hard, etc., if in the end you don't reach your quota or other numerical sales targets. Twenty years of *unsuccessful* sales experience does not make you an appealing hire for a Sales organization.

CHAPTER SIXTEEN

Sales Engineering

Salespeople in tech companies are hired for their ability to sell, not for their sophisticated technical knowledge. But to sell complex technology – especially to highly technical buyers – someone needs to provide technical knowledge to both the prospect and to the salesperson. That's where Sales Engineers come in.

Sales Engineers – "SEs" as they are usually called, but also called Pre-Sales Consultants or Solutions Engineers – do not focus exclusively on technical product issues. More generally, they bridge the gap between a customer's business needs and their technical needs. In a sense, SEs are translators, matching up business needs with the best technical solution given the products' capabilities.

Note that the term "engineer" is misleading. Although most SEs do have an engineering or Computer Science degree, SEs do not "engineer" anything from scratch in the usual sense of the term.

What They Do

The primary role of an SE is to serve as a technical product consultant to both the salesperson and to the prospect. Among other things, this includes answering prospects' questions about product capabilities, creating technically focused slides for a sales presentation, leading sales discussions with technical staff members of the prospective customer, and responding to the technical portion of RFPs and RFIs (Request for Proposals or Request for Information).

Of course, SEs don't always know the answer to every product question. They thus usually serve as a single point of contact for technical issues in a sales cycle but will leverage the internal knowledge resources of their company to find the answers. SEs call upon Product Managers quite extensively, for instance. The further along a sales cycle is, the more the SE will be involved. Most SEs receive a modest sales commissions for their assistance in closing deals.

Another key role SEs play is demonstrating the product to prospective customers. The type of "demo" and the extent to which it is customized for a particular prospect varies based on the type of product and on the prospect's needs. For example, since websites are easy to customize in a demonstration mode, an SE at a vendor of Internet-based software might heavily customize a demo. Packaged software is trickier to customize, so perhaps only a handful of tweaks would be made. Hardware demos may involve configuring the hardware in a special way.

At some companies, the demo serves as the basis for the product that will ultimately be delivered to the customer. In this respect, the demo may be more analogous to a proof of concept, involving an actual deployment of software or installation of hardware. In these situations, the SE will typically work closely with Deployment or Engineering teams to build a quick-and-dirty but functional prototype. That prototype may then become the baseline configuration for the product that is ultimately deployed for the customer, and the SE may be hands-on involved in this deployment.

SEs may also provide valuable input into competitive analysis, which is typically managed by a Product Marketer, Product Manager or a dedicated Competitive Analyst. SEs are often asked detailed product questions by prospects regarding how their product compares to those of certain competitors. By exploring these questions, SEs learn valuable insights about their competitors' product capabilities. SEs also provide formal or informal training to their salespeople on what they're learning about their competitors' product capabilities and positioning.

At some companies, particularly smaller hardware companies, an SE might be involved in the entire sales, deployment, and even post-deployment experience for a customer. Before the sale, the SE might actually help the customer evaluate their products (even competitors' products!) and install software or hardware for the customer to evaluate (this is generally called a "sandbox") before committing to a purchase. During the deployment phase, the SE might help the company's deployment team install and configure the products purchased, and even train the customer on its use. Post-deployment, the SE might serve as a technical support resource should the customer experience any problems.

Useful Skills

The type of background a Sales Engineer needs for a given company depends on what kind of product the company makes and how technical the buyer is. For example, a company that sells semiconductor design automation software to electrical engineers will need SEs who have a degree in Computer Science or Electrical Engineering. In contrast, a company that makes sales automation software which is sold to sales managers might find that hiring an SE who previously worked with this software would have sufficient product knowledge and be able to "talk shop" with the customer.

Regardless of one's specific educational or professional backgrounds, the skills *all* SEs need include:

- The ability to translate customers' business needs into a technical solution that the company can provide.
- The ability to explain the company's product capabilities in terms that all parties at the customer who are involved in the purchase decision will understand and find compelling.
- Sufficient familiarity with the types of products made by the company to know what is and isn't possible to accomplish, whether by using out-of-the-box functionality, customization, or custom product development. Most newly hired SEs go through some kind of training program to get them up to speed on the company's product capabilities.
- Willingness to travel frequently, and often on short notice.

One of the more challenging job aspects for many SEs is remembering that they're part of the Sales team. Even though the SE isn't a salesperson, what he or she says and does in a sales cycle has a *direct* impact on whether the company wins the deal. Many SEs have technical backgrounds and find themselves working with technical employees at the prospective customer. It's easy for those discussions to get "down in the weeds" on technical topics, and SEs strive to be open and honest with their counterparts – sometimes too much so. SEs need to be good at positioning their company and its product in the best possible light, even if the truth is that the product has limitations. To these ends, a background in Sales can be very helpful. One company's job description for an SE put it well: "Your ability to evoke confidence in our solutions and technology infrastructure to overcome all technical objections in the sales cycle is essential."

Career Paths

Sales Engineering is seldom an entry-level role. Prior to becoming an SE, most individuals gained expertise with the company's product at the company in another department, such as engineering or product development (where they designed the product), information technology (where they administered the product), technical support (where they supported the product), or professional services (where they deployed the product). Some SEs come from other companies (sometimes customers), where they gained product expertise by using the product there, or something similar to it.

Many people are attracted to sales engineering because, despite a background in something other than sales, they find it more conducive to their personality or financial goals. Although the base salaries for SEs may be lower than those for engineering positions, with sales commissions and bonuses an SE may earn far more in total compensation.

Others are attracted to the field because of geographic flexibility. Since most SEs travel extensively to customer sites and can often do their work anywhere there is an Internet connection, it usually doesn't matter where they're based.

To get into Sales Engineering, the best advice is to become a product expert on the company's products or something similar to them. Also, become comfortable working with a Sales organization and learn about the art and science of the selling process.

Sales Engineering is great preparation for a variety of other careers within tech, such as becoming a Product Manager, joining a Professional Services team in a new customer deployment capacity, or as a Consultant of various types. Because SEs understand the sales process and the product so well, sales engineering is also a good foundation for Marketing leadership positions.

CHAPTER SEVENTEEN

Sales Operations

Operations is a catch-all phrase that denotes the tactical, day-to-day processes that make a company run. The term is most often used in a manufacturing context, where Operations involves managing a supply chain – getting materials and finished goods to the right place at the right time. In the context of sales in a tech company, it's something completely different: providing decision support and tactical assistance to those who manage the sales process.

Sales Operations staff are usually not brought in to a company until the company crosses a certain size threshold. This threshold varies by company, but generally it's whenever the need for more sophisticated data collection and analysis about the Sales function becomes apparent. This usually correlates with the point at which the Sales team grows large enough that it becomes complicated to manage.

What They Do

The specific activities in which Sales Operations Managers (SOMs) are engaged vary extensively from company to company. At a high level, SOMs typically have two primary roles: providing the quantitative data and analysis that enables the entire Sales department to function efficiently, and arming the Sales team with productivity-enhancing technology tools. In addition, SOMs often get involved in sales-related "special projects" that don't fit neatly into the usual assigned roles for other Sales and Marketing personnel.

SOMs usually report to a senior Sales Director or directly to the VP of Sales, and as such are frequently called upon to provide ad-hoc reports to facilitate decision making. To illustrate the range of data collection and analysis that SOMs might get involved in, it helps to think about some of the information needs of executives in Sales and other departments:

- Which salesperson do I assign to which territory?
- What quota do I assign to each salesperson?
- How will I track the performance of each salesperson against his or her quota, or the performance of my entire team?
- My Board of Directors wants to know how much my team can sell next quarter.
- My Chief Financial Officer wants to know how much I expect to pay my team in sales commissions next year.
- The CFO also wants to know what deals were the most profitable – that is, generated the highest revenue at the lowest cost of sales.
- The VP of Marketing wants to know how many deals we lost to our major competitors last year.
- Product Marketing wants to know if the official price list is "working." Is Sales discounting heavily from list prices? Are some products seemingly underpriced?
- Our investors want to know what our average deal size is, and if it's increasing or decreasing over time.

- Sales managers want to know how many deals are at each stage of the sales process, and how long they've been there.

To compile such information, SOMs typically work closely with Finance, Accounting, and Legal staff members and, to a lesser extent, with the Marketing team. Most SOMs will set up automated processes to gather and report on important metrics (sometimes called Key Performance Indicators, or KPIs) to the executive team at weekly, monthly or quarterly intervals.

Another common role for SOMs is to work with internal IT (information technology) groups to provide the Sales team with various technical tools to make their jobs easier and more productive. This may include so-called sales force automation (SFA) software tools (the most popular of which is Salesforce.com), proposal or price quote generation software, and contact management software, among others. SOMs may be involved in any combination of the vendor selection or software implementation process, training the Sales team on using the tools, or the ongoing maintenance and administration of these tools.

Many SOMs also are involved to some extent in training the Sales team – particularly new hires – on sales policies and processes.

SOMs frequently are the liaison between Sales and other departments. If, for example, a software company customer is disputing its billed charges, Accounting may work with the SOM to review the contract signed, the SOM may then work with the customer's Account Manager to discuss the points of contention, and the SOM may work with Legal to plan a contingency course of action.

Useful Skills

SOMs need to have a broad base of skills, as they will be working with individuals from multiple departments. General knowledge or experience of tech company sales processes is important, but equally important is a solid foundation of understanding of accounting, finance, and legal principles. In lieu of experience in these areas, a Bachelor's or Master's degree in Accounting or Finance would be valuable. Coursework in business law, particularly contracts, could be useful, too.

SOM roles are highly quantitative, so you should be comfortable with math and basic statistics. You also should be comfortable transforming large amounts of raw numerical data into tables and graphs that help your internal audiences quickly digest it.

You should be a wizard at using Microsoft Excel. General familiarity with using software tools could be helpful, too, especially if you will be working with IT on selecting or implementing productivity-enhancing tools for the Sales team.

Finally, you should be comfortable working with senior management. Your analytical skills will occasionally be called upon by executives throughout the company to guide their decision making.

Career Paths

There is no common entry point into an SOM role. Most SOMs have a degree in Finance, Accounting or another Business area, and usually fall into an SOM role somewhat inadvertently after working in a related area for a few years, such as in a Finance or Accounting group. Experience in tech, specifically, is generally desired by employers but rarely required.

Sales Ops is rarely an entry-level role. Most individuals begin at the Manager level and some larger companies have a team of SOMs with a Director leading the team. A VP level position in Sales Ops is quite rare.

If you're interested in Sales Ops, a good strategy is to begin working with or within a Sales department, in any capacity, in any industry. This will help you understand how Sales departments function. And if you're not already well-versed in software tools like Microsoft Excel and Salesforce.com, take courses or read instructional books to get better acquainted with these. Depending on your academic or professional background, you may also find coursework in basic accounting, finance and statistics to be helpful, as well.

Glossary

The tech industry is full of jargon. Below are simple definitions of some terms you are likely to encounter as you research tech companies. For even more definitions, visit the Resources section of www.TechJobsBook.com.

C-Level The highest level ("Chief") job titles in any company, most commonly including CEO (Chief Executive Officer), CFO (Chief Financial Officer), CTO (Chief Technology Officer), and CMO (Chief Marketing Officer).

Collateral Marketing materials that are primarily geared toward prospective customers for use in a sales cycle. Examples include brochures, product data/fact sheets, whitepapers, and guides of various kinds. This term has nothing to do with the legal definition of collateral, meaning property that secures a loan.

Direct reports Individuals whose work is directed and evaluated by a more senior individual. Usually used in context by the person to whom the others report, e.g., "My direct reports include the three people in Product Marketing."

FAQ Frequently Asked Questions. Many marketers create documents or website copy (text on a website) referred to as FAQs that attempt to break down complicated information into a more digestible question-and-answer format.

Horizontal In the context of a tech company, this usually refers to a product or product line. Product Marketers and Product Managers usually "own" certain "horizontals." Also see *Segment* and *Vertical*.

Market In tech companies, this term usually refers to the industry that the company competes in (e.g., "We make products for the semiconductor test equipment market"). *A target market* is an industry that the company sells to.

MBA Master (or Master's) of Business Administration. A two year graduate level course of study in business. Many tech companies seek MBAs because of the perception that they have a well-rounded business education.

Out-of-the-box Software or hardware that either cannot or does not necessarily need to be customized or modified in any way to meet a particular customer's needs.

RFP/RFI/RFQ Requests for Proposals, Information, or Quotes, respectively. These are documents issued by a prospective corporate buyer to prospective vendors. These requests outline the buyer's needs and seek feedback in a well-defined format.

Sales cycle The entire process of selling a product or service, beginning with some form of initial engagement with a prospective customer (such as a phone call from the prospect to enquire about pricing) until the point when the customer signs a contract with the company or informs the selling company that they will not purchase anything. For tech companies, sales cycles can last from a few days to a year or more, depending on the complexity and price of the product, the ability for the customer to secure budget for the product, and many other factors.

Segment Similar to the term *vertical* (meaning "an industry"), but usually on a more granular level. If "telecom" is the vertical, segments might include telecom hardware, telecom software, telecom services, and so on. As with the term *vertical*, this term is used in the context of which markets a company pursues.

Space Tech company jargon for the industry in which the company sells. Common usage examples are, "Our company is in the enterprise software space," or, "We play in the Web 2.0 space." This is just another term for *market* or *industry*.

Vertical Another word for "industry," such as aerospace, automotive, manufacturing, telecom, etc. This term is often used in the context of, "This product is targeted at the following verticals."

Webinar A seminar conducted remotely over the Web. The "audience" views the slides through their Web browser and hears the speaker's commentary over their telephone. Conducting a webinar is much less expensive than holding an in-person seminar and can reach a much larger audience (the entire Internet-enabled world).

Whitepaper Also commonly spelled with two words, a whitepaper is a document that explores a theme or narrow topic in some depth (usually 5-25 pages). An example: "What You Need to Know About Content Management Systems." Whitepapers are partly an educational tool and partly an advertisement for a company's products. They typically include a useful primer on a topic but then lead the reader to conclude that the company that wrote the paper is clearly the best vendor.

About the Author

David Wolpert has worked in product marketing, product management, market development, field marketing, and partnerships and alliances for small, privately held software companies, publicly traded Internet companies, and for VC-backed, mid-sized companies.

This is his third book. His first book – *Scoliosis Surgery: The Definitive Patient's Reference* – is now in its third edition. He also co-authored *The Human Fabric: Unleashing the Power of Core Energy in Everyone*. Both are available on Amazon.com.

David holds a B.S. in History from Carnegie Mellon University and an M.B.A. from the University of Texas. A native of Detroit, today David resides in Austin.

Printed in Great Britain
by Amazon

21236555R00088